CITY CRITTERS

Wildlife in the Urban Jungle

NICHOLAS READ

ORCA BOOK PUBLISHERS

Library and Archives Canada Cataloguing in Publication

Read, Nicholas, 1956-
City critters : wildlife in the urban jungle /
written by Nicholas Read.

Issued also in an electronic format.
ISBN 978-1-55469-394-8

1. Urban animals--Juvenile literature. I. Title.

QH541.5.C6R43 2012   J591.75'6   C2011-907424-9

First published in the United States, 2012
Library of Congress Control Number: 2011942577

Summary: An entertaining and informative look at the many wild animals that share the North American urban environment.

Orca Book Publishers is dedicated to preserving the environment and has printed this book on paper certified by the Forest Stewardship Council.®

Orca Book Publishers gratefully acknowledges the support for its publishing programs provided by the following agencies: the Government of Canada through the Canada Book Fund and the Canada Council for the Arts, and the Province of British Columbia through the BC Arts Council and the Book Publishing Tax Credit.

Cover design by Teresa Bubela
Interior layout and illustrations by Jasmine Devonshire
Front cover photography by Michael Durham/Getty Images
Back cover photography by, from left, *Vancouver Sun*, US National Park Service,
Cathy Keifer/Dreamstime.com, William Osler Health System (Etobicoke General Hospital, Etobicoke, Ontario),
Laura Cox, Christian Laub, Laura Cox, Doreen Gray and Kay Steer.

ORCA BOOK PUBLISHERS
PO Box 5626, Stn. B
Victoria, BC CANADA
V8R 6S4

ORCA BOOK PUBLISHERS
PO Box 468
Custer, WA USA
98240-0468

www.orcabook.com
Printed and bound in Canada.

15 14 13 12 • 4 3 2 1

To those brave few who still have faith enough to spit into the wind

Contents

OPPOSITE: The world for wildlife is getting less natural all the time. So sometimes animals need a little help...from us. Someone dropped a chunk of apple, which this chipmunk very gratefully picked up and ate. DREAMSTIME.COM

Introduction
Wildlife in the Urban Jungle

You and your family probably live in a city. Maybe it's a big city. Or maybe it's a town or a suburb. Maybe only a couple of thousand people share it with you, or maybe it's a huge metropolis like Los Angeles or Toronto. New York, the biggest metropolis in America, has more than 20 million people in it. That's gigantic. But big or small—20 million or 2,000—you probably live in an urban area with streets, houses, malls and cars. Statistics say 80 percent of American children live in places like this. In Canada the number's even higher. So it's very likely that right now, as you open this book, you're in some form of a city too.

But if you look carefully, you'll see that more than just people share your city. Out your window there may be a starling about to take flight. In your basement you might find a spider spinning a web. Or in your backyard a squirrel might be scampering from tree to tree. Look past the houses, malls and cars, and you'll probably see other animals too: raccoons, skunks, foxes, pigeons, sparrows and crows, to name a few. You may not

OPPOSITE: If there were a poster species for North America's urban wildlife, it likely would be the raccoon. They're found almost everywhere on the continent. DREAMSTIME.COM

1

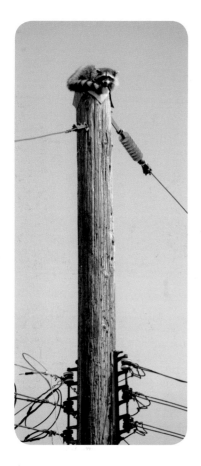

ABOVE: Because they are so adaptable, raccoons will turn up almost anywhere in a city. This one found her way to the top of a telephone pole.

GLENN BAGLO/VANCOUVER SUN

see them all the time—some are nocturnal, so they only come out at night—but that doesn't mean they're not there.

Animals like these have become permanent residents in cities throughout the United States and Canada. They've moved into places we used to think of as belonging to people and no one else. The strange thing is that for a long time they did it without anyone noticing. It's like that expression, "Now you see them, now you don't," only in reverse. Now we can't help noticing them because they're everywhere. Even in Beverly Hills, one of the swankiest neighborhoods on the continent, residents are advised to protect their pets from coyotes who come down from the Hollywood Hills to hunt.

Of course, the types of animals you encounter in cities will depend on the city you live in. Alligators, who need to be warm, wouldn't last a day in Denver in December. But if the thought of finding one in a backyard swimming pool terrifies you, you'd better not move to Miami. Other animals—those ever-present raccoons, skunks, squirrels and coyotes among them—tend to turn up everywhere. And people are starting to wonder why.

Not long ago, things were different. Twenty or so years ago, it was possible to let your cat outside without worrying that it would be snatched by a wolflike creature with forty-two teeth and a taste for antelope. Even now, it sounds far-fetched that such an animal, a coyote, would roam the streets of a place like Chicago. But as anyone who's lost a pet cat or small dog to one will tell you, it's not. Studies suggest that more than 2,000 coyotes live in and around the Windy City, along with about 9 million people. Wildlife—what we now call **urban wildlife** (words in **bold** can be found in the Glossary on page 126)—has become a fact of life in North American cities, even those as vast as Chicago. Cities are not just for people anymore.

Not that they ever were, at least not in the strictest sense. They've always been home to rats. Throughout history, wherever people have gone, rats have gone too. So have mice. Both eat the crumbs people leave behind. And there have always been songbirds. The "robin red breast" (actually the American robin) has long been a familiar harbinger of spring in many North American cities. Insects, too, are an enduring part of urban life. What would a picnic in the park be without a battalion of ants?

What is new is that many cities are now home to different kinds of wildlife, wildlife that used to live only where you'd think wildlife would live: in wilderness. Years ago, it was unheard of for a black bear to navigate anything but the mountains north of Vancouver, or for a white-tailed deer to dodge traffic and dogs for a geranium dinner in Boston. Now those deer are as common as dandelions. Bears less so, but in certain city suburbs they make regular appearances each spring and summer. Even cougars show up occasionally. The question is, why?

Within Chicago's famed Lincoln Park Zoo, a group called the Urban Wildlife Institute is trying to find out. It has enlisted scientists from a number of different disciplines to study urban wildlife and how it is able to live so near to us. One of the institute's aims is to find out how we and wildlife can get along better, because more and more people now realize we have to try.

Years ago when urban raccoons, skunks and coyotes began appearing in larger numbers, city officials thought they could get rid of them by killing them. They were wrong. In addition to being cruel, killing individual animals proved to have no impact on overall populations. If a homeowner poisoned

TOP: Urban wildlife comes in all sizes— from the largest moose to the smallest mouse. WAYNE CAMPBELL

BOTTOM: Though songbirds aren't nearly as common in urban skies as they once were, many species, including the American robin, continue to cling on. WANDA UNDERHILL

TOP: The coyote, perhaps more than any other kind of urban animal, has transformed many urban landscapes. RIC ERNST/THE PROVINCE

BOTTOM: Because of urban sprawl, black bears are being displaced from their traditional territories in parts of Canada and the northern United States. This one found his way into a Vancouver dump truck just before Christmas 2011. JAMES GEMMIL

a raccoon in his or her backyard, it wouldn't be long before another raccoon took the first one's place. If coyotes in a particular neighborhood suffered an especially high death rate, females would simply have more pups to replace them.

Now we've learned that, like it or not, certain kinds of wildlife have decided to call North American cities home too. And there's nothing we humans can do about it. As the old saying goes, "If we can't beat 'em, we may as well join 'em"—because they've decided to join us. That's why the Chicago institute is now studying conflicts between wildlife and people, diseases that can be passed between the two (AIDS, West Nile virus and the avian flu all originated in animals), and the territories we share. They believe what they learn in Chicago can be of benefit throughout North America.

But how did we reach a point where having a black bear in your garden, while never desirable (for you or the bear), has become almost normal? Believe it or not, you can probably answer the question in one word: space. There isn't enough of it anymore. Not for the world's wild animals and all 7 billion (and counting) of us.

The sad truth is that this is a terrible time to be a wild animal. All over the world, wild creatures of every size, shape and stripe are becoming extinct. Rhinos are disappearing from Kenya. Tigers are vanishing from India. Orangutans are fading from Indonesia. Here in North America, grizzly bears live only in fragments of Idaho, Wyoming and Alberta as well as larger portions of British Columbia and Alaska. We are in the midst of what scientists call "the sixth great extinction," meaning this is the sixth time in geological history that huge numbers of animal species have disappeared in a very short period of time. The last one occurred about 65 million years ago when, it's believed, either an asteroid or a comet struck the Earth and wiped out the dinosaurs. This time the **extinction** can't be blamed on an outside event. It's our fault and no one else's.

Thousands of animal species disappear from the Earth every year, so in a hundred years—a mere blink in geological time—who knows how many will be left? The world is only so big, and there simply isn't room in it for all the animals and us, especially when we live the way we do in North America—in big houses on big lots with big roads to serve them. So wild animals, who need large tracts of wilderness to survive, are paying the price.

At least most are, but not all. Some animals—such as those raccoons, skunks, squirrels and coyotes—have been lucky, or clever, enough to figure out a way to make our homes their homes too. They've been able to beat the odds and survive. Their secret is a process called **adaptation**.

Humans are remarkably adaptable creatures. If you had to move to a new home or school and learn a whole new set of subjects, you probably wouldn't like it, but over time you'd get used to it. Even if you had to move to a brand-new city or country, you'd adjust. You'd probably feel out of place at first ("like a fish out of water," as the saying goes), but with enough time, that feeling would pass. You may never learn to like your new city or country, but you'd get used to it. You'd adapt.

ABOVE: Deer have become so common in some North American suburbs that they'll turn up even on the busiest freeway. RAYMOND GEHMAN/ NATIONAL GEOGRAPHIC

Most animals can't. They've evolved to live in a particular way in a particular place. If that place—their **habitat**—is destroyed, they die. This is the main reason so many kinds of animals are vanishing: not because they're being hunted or trapped in large numbers (although those are big problems too) but because their habitats—the forests, jungles, marshes and

grasslands they live in—are being destroyed. Polar bears can't live without massive ice floes on which to hunt, so if the floes melt, as they are around the North Pole, the bears will die. If the African forests where mountain gorillas live are cut down to stumps, as many are, the gorillas will die too. There's a direct and unbreakable connection between where an animal lives and how it lives.

There are some wild animals, however, who are more like humans in that if their habitats are destroyed or altered, they will still survive. Biologists call these animals "**generalists**" because, as the name suggests, they're not as picky about where and how they live. All the raccoons, skunks, squirrels, possums and coyotes who've come to live alongside humans in North American cities are generalists. They've all adapted to an entirely new living place. They've managed to move successfully from the wilderness into a city—a move that would kill other kinds of creatures, including most large **carnivores**. When cities spread out into suburbs and **exurbs** (suburbs beyond suburbs) and wilderness is destroyed, large meat eaters like wolves and cougars can't cope. Yes, cougars do appear now and then in city suburbs, but only briefly and only if there's wilderness nearby. Wolves never appear. Nature's generalists aren't as specialized in their needs. As long as there's some green space left—and when you think about it, there's plenty thanks to all the gardens, parks, golf courses and even cemeteries in cities—they manage.

In fact, in some ways generalists may be better off in cities than they are in the wilderness. When the **predators** who eat them (those wolves and cougars) or compete with them (as coyotes do) are not around anymore, life gets easier. Yes, they still have to worry about being hit by cars, the most dangerous predator of all, but they don't have to worry about becoming somebody else's dinner. So they have more time to search for their own. It takes a lot of fuel to be constantly on guard against a creature who might eat you, but if that creature is no longer there, you can use the energy you'd otherwise have spent running for your life on improving it: on gathering food, searching for places to build nests and dens, mating and raising young. So it could be that life is easier for urban wildlife. Without being able to ask them, we can't know for sure, but it does make you wonder.

ABOVE: Cities present urban critters with all kinds of dangers, but somehow they manage to survive. This chipmunk is proof of that. AMBER HOBBS/ ATD PHOTOGRAPHY

When it comes to finding food, a city can be a dining table for urban wildlife. Huge supplies of food are trucked into cities every day because there are so many people in them to feed. But unlike nature, which wastes nothing, human beings in modern urban jungles waste almost everything: energy, water, soil, building materials and food. We waste colossal amounts of food. If you doubt that, check out the number of overflowing

ABOVE: Bald eagles, the proud symbol of the United States, are remarkably resilient birds. As such, they can be found in the unlikeliest of places, including tire lots. WAYNE CAMPBELL

garbage bins after a sporting event or a public gathering like a parade or fireworks display. Check out the Dumpster behind any restaurant. Check out your own waste bins. How much dinner did you toss out last night?

Food is everywhere in a city. A lot of it is food wild animals were never supposed to eat, such as French fries and chicken nuggets. (Humans were never supposed to eat them either, although we do.) But one of the defining characteristics of generalists is that they'll eat almost anything. Humans are generalists too. Yes, we all have our favorite dishes, but we eat a whole range of foods, from vegetables to fruit to meat to milk to cereal, and everything that can be made out of those foods too.

In contrast, many other animals can eat only one type of food, or at least a very narrow range of foods. They're what biologists call **specialists**. The world's large cats—lions, tigers, leopards, cheetahs, jaguars and cougars—are dedicated carnivores, meaning they have to have fresh meat to survive. Wolves are the same; without meat, they'll die. Pandas, the black-and-white bears who live in China's temperate forests, eat almost nothing but bamboo. In fact, bamboo makes up

Amazing Animal Adaptation

Bald eagles, America's national symbol, will build nests in city trees. When their chicks are born, they appear to be completely indifferent to any and all kinds of noisy human activity, providing that activity doesn't threaten the chicks or their chances of being fed. Several pairs have even built nests in Philadelphia, which is appropriate since Philadelphia was once America's capital.

Peregrine falcons in the wild build their nests on cliffs, but cliffs are rare in cities, so a pair of peregrines living in New York City built their nest at the top of the next best thing—the city's famous Brooklyn Bridge. In Chicago, a pair has built their nest on the roof of a thirty-one-story building on Wacker Drive in the heart of downtown. Farther north, in Edmonton, a third peregrine falcon pair has built their nest on top of the clinical sciences building at the University of Alberta. Smart birds!

99 percent of everything they put in their mouths (the rest is made up of other kinds of grass and the occasional small rodent). What could be more specialized than that?

But generalists can eat a whole range of foods, including the foods city-dwelling humans throw out in such huge quantities every day. That's not to say coyotes eat French fries, but the animals coyotes eat—rats, mice, voles and other small rodents—will. Or if they won't eat French fries, they'll eat enough of what humans eat and throw away to survive, even thrive. So they multiply and have rat, mouse, vole and other small rodent young. That makes urban coyotes happy because the more small rodents there are in a city, the more coyote dinners there are too.

Birds of prey, called **raptors**, have the same kind of relationship with crows, pigeons and sparrows. Crows, pigeons and sparrows also eat a lot of the foods humans throw away. Think of how eagerly a flock of pigeons will peck at a handful

ABOVE: The sight of an urban deer used to be something extraordinary. Now, with deer numbers exploding, even domestic cats aren't fazed by them. GERDA KNUFF

of spilled bread crumbs. As crows, pigeons and sparrows have become flying fixtures in cities all over North America, so have certain birds of prey. Red-tailed hawks and peregrine falcons won't eat bread crumbs, but they will eat smaller birds who do. So the more bread crumbs there are for small birds to eat, the more small birds there are for raptors to hunt. And that means more raptors in the urban sky.

Generalists also aren't fussy about where they build nests or dens. Raccoons and skunks will build a den in a basement or an attic because everything they need for one is there: warmth, dryness and privacy. And if there's a family of six humans charging around downstairs getting in and out of their SUV on their way to and from soccer practice, who cares? Curiously, that would freak out bigger, fiercer animals. You wouldn't catch a grizzly bear being so accommodating—it would be outta there like a hunter's bullet.

Our changing climate is also having an effect. Almost every year, the world gets a little warmer. This is especially true in cities because cities trap heat. All the concrete, glass, tar and other materials that go into constructing a city's roads and buildings absorb and retain heat. Add to that all the exhaust belching from millions of tailpipes every day, and cities become a heat sink. This trapped heat can create some desperately uncomfortable summers for people, but in winter it's a blessing, especially for certain kinds of animals. Many bird species are supposed to fly south in winter to escape Canada's—and much of midwestern and northeastern America's—harsh winters. That's how they evolved. But when winters aren't as punishing as they used to be, and when people leave food in urban parks for them to peck at year-round, the birds stay put. Why expend all that energy to fly south when they can stay up north and be fine?

ABOVE: Coyotes have always been a staple of the California landscape. Now they're even found in Beverly Hills.
ROB MCKAY/DREAMSTIME.COM

Finally, people who live in cities tend to feel increasingly indifferent to having wild animals in them too. That's important because it means urban wildlife no longer have to worry about being killed intentionally. Of course, there are exceptions. People with cats or small dogs wish there weren't so many coyotes. And who likes being dive-bombed by a pair of angry crows? Canada geese deposit ugly droppings on lawns, and skunks leave pungent calling cards on fences, lampposts and dogs. In Florida, alligators turn up on golf courses at the most inopportune times. (Is there an opportune time for an alligator to appear?) And urban deer have a way of choosing the most beautiful and fragrant plants in a garden to nibble on.

But as annoyed as we might be with them, we rarely go out of our way to harm them. We may hit them accidentally with our cars, and occasionally we'll call pest control companies to remove them from our properties. Every now and then angry citizen patrols will discuss culling large flocks of Canada geese or hungry herds of urban deer. At the University of Victoria in British Columbia, officials wrestled for years with the problem of rabbits burrowing under the campus's lawns and gardens. But by and large we've come to terms with urban wildlife. And that's good news for them.

This book will introduce you to some of that wildlife—the familiar and not-so-familiar urban critters who share our urban jungle. It will explain where they live, how they live and how we can live more peaceably with them. Because, remember, there's only so much world to go around, and with cities taking up more and more of it all the time, city living is fast becoming one of the best and only ways for some wildlife to survive.

How aware are people becoming of urban wildlife?

There's plenty of evidence to suggest people are thinking about urban wildlife more than ever before. Certainly there's more scientific inquiry, including that done by the US National Science Foundation, which has established urban research sites in Baltimore and Phoenix and funded an awards program for research into urban forests and the natural resources therein. There are also more scientific publications about urban wildlife. From 1993 to 1998, fewer than one in a hundred of the articles that appeared in the world's nine most prestigious **ecology** journals dealt with cities and urban species. In the last five years, the number has grown sixfold, and it's increasing all the time. In 1992, only one item about **urban ecology** was presented to the Ecological Society of America's annual meeting. In 2010, there were 202. Mentions of urban coyotes in US newspapers have also increased: in 1990, there were two; last year, there were more than 250.

Chapter One

Hair, Teeth and Eyes— The Mammals

When we think of deer, many of us picture Bambi— a graceful, timid creature who nibbles delicately on forest leaves and leaps away at the first sign of danger. So it was with jaws dropped and eyes open wide that people watched a doe like Bambi's mom attack a dog in the small British Columbia town of Cranbrook (search "deer attacks dog" on YouTube). The deer thought her fawn was being threatened, so she went after the dog with hooves flying, kicking and stomping him in a way you'd expect to see in a WWE wrestling ring, not a small-town side street. Fortunately, the dog, who was pretty old and frail, wasn't hurt, but people were shocked. Viewers just couldn't get over seeing a deer, an animal they picture one way, behaving so outrageously in another. No wonder the video went viral, getting almost three million hits.

Shortly after, a newspaper carrier in the same town complained of being head-butted by another deer. "I was just lucky it was the head because their hooves are so sharp," Brock James said afterward. He suffered a gash in his chin that required

OPPOSITE: Rats are the ultimate urban mammal. Wherever people go, rats follow. MICHAEL DURHAM/MINDEN PICTURES/NATIONAL GEOGRAPHIC

TOP: Despite their size, moose have much to fear from people, especially people behind the wheel of a car.
LAURA COX

BOTTOM: Deer have become so numerous in some urban areas that citizens want them culled. It's a controversial business, to say the least.
THEA HAUBRICH

eight stitches to close. The following year in Langley, a suburb of Vancouver, a mother doe protecting her fawn stomped on an elderly dog and broke her back. The dog had to be put down.

All over the United States and Canada, white-tailed deer, once known best as the endearing stars of that classic 1942 Disney cartoon, are becoming targets of city dwellers fed up with seeing their gardens browsed to bits. In some US states, the problem is considered serious enough for lawmakers to permit hunting of urban deer with rifles and crossbows. In Canada, such "control" measures are usually left to government. Regardless, it's an issue, with more and more people thinking about deer in a way they never have before—because deer are going places they've never gone before.

What happened? As mentioned in the Introduction, it's a question of space: ours and theirs. As cities grow bigger and more sprawling, wilderness areas get smaller and more limited, so what's a doe, buck or fawn to do except go for those petunias in your flower bed? After all, the deer don't know they were cultivated specially to decorate that dead space between the front path and the window box. To deer they're just food. We shouldn't blame them, but we do. So when deer like the ones in Cranbrook and Langley get frightened and defend their offspring in the same way they would in the wild, we freak. We demand that "something" be done, and, chances are, whatever that something is will be bad for the deer.

Such is the curious relationship we have with large urban mammals. We may like the idea of deer, moose, bears, cougars, bobcats and coyotes roaming the hills around the cities where we live. Knowing they're there gives us a connection to nature that city living undercuts. But once they move out of those hills and into our neighborhoods, we think differently. On one hand, it's kind of cool to see a deer or bear so close to where we live. After all, they're not supposed to be there, and a lot of us have a soft spot for rule breakers. But on the other hand, they really are not supposed to be there, and sometimes they cause trouble. Deer destroy gardens. Bears, moose and large cats can hurt people and damage property, and coyotes hunt our beloved cats and dogs. So when you look at it that way, the idea of living so close to nature isn't quite so appealing.

But again, we've given nature—and especially those large animals—little choice. When we destroy the wilderness they rely on, we deny them the life nature intended them to live. And that condemns them to a life where they get into trouble. In the wild, deer populations are checked by large predators, mainly cougars and wolves. But in urban areas where there are no big predators, there's nothing to keep deer populations under control, except people—with guns and crossbows.

Unlike deer, urban moose are rare in most places, but if you live in a small city or town in northern Canada or Alaska, they're as common as a white Christmas. This makes sense when you consider that all these northern towns were built smack in the middle of moose habitat. Moose are very large, so they can do a lot of damage to a car or truck if one hits them. Passengers may be injured too. This is a hazard in towns where moose are prevalent. Yet in such collisions it's often the moose who suffers most. Many die.

Urban moose are a particular problem in the Canadian province of Newfoundland, where, in 1878 and again in 1904, people introduced breeding pairs to a place moose were never meant to be. Once there was a species of wolf in Newfoundland too,

✏ Mammals on the fringe

Three medium-sized mammals seen inside urban borders from time to time are beavers, mink and foxes. But unlike coyotes, skunks or raccoons, beavers, mink and foxes never parade down city streets or poke their noses in city gardens. If they're found in cities, it's usually because of an urban park system big and natural enough to meet their special needs. Beavers require trees and ponds to live—trees to cut down and ponds in which to build lodges. And it's the rare urban park that's prepared to suffer that kind of damage. Mink require freshwater swamps, known as **wetlands**, to survive. But wetlands are among the most endangered habitats in the world, especially in cities. So if there's no mink habitat, there are no mink.

Urban fox territories include golf courses, parks and some suburban areas, as long as the houses are spread out and there aren't too many people. In Europe urban foxes are everywhere. In Great Britain they're as common as pubs. But in North America urban living isn't the lure for foxes that it is there.

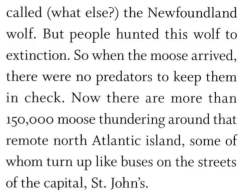

ABOVE: The presence of black bears on urban streets depends largely on how much food there is for them in the wilderness. If there isn't enough, they'll look for it elsewhere. TOM BOPPART

called (what else?) the Newfoundland wolf. But people hunted this wolf to extinction. So when the moose arrived, there were no predators to keep them in check. Now there are more than 150,000 moose thundering around that remote north Atlantic island, some of whom turn up like buses on the streets of the capital, St. John's.

Urban bears face similar dangers. As soon as a bear grows accustomed to getting its dinner from someone's fruit tree or garbage can, that bear is in trouble. **Conservation officers** will either relocate it or pull out a rifle. But with cities spreading farther out into bear territories all the time, it's no surprise that bears and backyards are getting together more often. Vancouver is a perfect example. Suburbs now extend high into perimeter mountains where black bears live. So people in those suburbs have grown accustomed to coming face-to-face with bears.

How often bears appear in these neighborhoods depends on how much food there is in what's left of the still-wild mountains. In a year when food is scarce, bears will move into urban areas if they think they can find something to eat. But in a year when the forest is full of berries, nuts and ant larvae—bears are crazy about ant larvae—people wonder where they went. Put simply: bears are smart. And adaptable. If they figure out that food is available in an urban backyard when the forest's larder is empty, they'll go to that backyard. When nature is generous, there's no need for them to head anywhere else, so they don't—unless there's a landfill nearby.

Landfills can be irresistible to bears because they're like a fast-food drive-through where the food is every bit as tasty—and bad for them—as junk food is for people. In fact, a study done near Lake Tahoe along the California/Nevada border

found that black bears living in urban areas weighed about 30 percent more than bears in the wild. Why? Because urban bears got their dinners from landfills where they ate leftover junk food, the same junk food people eat. And just as it does in people, junk food makes bears fat and lazy. Researchers found that because there was so much junk food in the landfill, and because bears found it so easy to gather, they didn't get any exercise foraging for it. And a fat, lazy bear who depends on a landfill for food is a bear who's gunning for trouble—in the form of a gun-toting conservation officer. Thousands of bears are killed in and around North American landfills every year because they've grown accustomed to eating from them, and in the minds of authorities, that's too close to many urban areas for comfort.

We rarely see big cats like cougars in cities, but that doesn't mean they're not there. Greater Los Angeles is a megacity of more than 13 million people, making it the second-largest

ABOVE: Cougars, or mountain lions, aren't nearly as at home in urban areas as other wildlife, but they will turn up occasionally on the fringes of cities to hunt. US NATIONAL PARK SERVICE

metropolis in the United States. Hardly a place you'd expect to find a 220-pound (100-kilogram) wild cat. But cougars, or mountain lions, live in the Santa Monica Mountains that surround LA, so sometimes they come down from those mountains to hunt.

Unlike deer and bears, though, cougars are reluctant to go far inside cities. One reason is that they appear to know people are trouble, so they stay away from them. Another is that their main food source is deer, and it's almost impossible to chase a deer around a swimming pool and a barbecue. It's much easier to go after them in the mountains, where all they have to avoid are rocks and trees. And unlike bears, cougars aren't interested in people's garbage, no matter how many leftover tacos it contains. So they never go through it.

Cougars are also accustomed to hunting in large territories. In the wilderness you never find them in confined spaces, so the chances of seeing one in an urban area are slim. After all, a cat with a big territory could be anywhere within that territory at any given time. Nevertheless, they've been spotted in Denver, Seattle, Tucson and Victoria, as well as Los Angeles. In the summer of 2011, four were sighted in Victoria. Two were a mother and cub wandering through a suburb at midday. Which goes to show that even cougars can't be counted out of today's urban wildlife mix.

Bobcats are another reluctant urban critter. They, too, prefer the wilderness, yet they're more common in residential areas than cougars because they eat animals that cougars don't—small animals such as rabbits. Bobcats love rabbits, and Los Angeles is hopping with them. Which is why you'll find bobcats in Los Angeles, as well as San Francisco, Tucson, Vancouver and, most famously, an island resort community off the coast of South Carolina called Kiawah Island. About 1,500 people live on Kiawah Island, and during the summer that number doubles or triples. Bobcats live there too, lots of them. They keep the rat, mouse and deer populations under control, and tourists are under strict instructions to leave them alone.

There is one fairly large predator who is perfectly at home in many cities: the coyote. There's hardly a city left in North America where you don't find them. Recently, one even found his way into Manhattan, the most densely populated piece of ground on the continent. Once again, the reason is that they're so adaptable. When nature throws them a curve ball, they know how to hit it back. In the wild, coyotes are both predators and **prey**. That is, they have to worry about being killed by bigger predators—wolves and cougars. In the city they don't.

TOP: Coyotes are now so common in North American cities that one was recently spotted in Manhattan, the densest urban area in the United States.
ARLEN REDEKOP/THE PROVINCE

BOTTOM: Coyotes feed on any number of urban rodents as well as domestic cats and small dogs.

ABOVE: The more food that's left out for raccoons, the bigger their families will grow. KATY THOMPSON

OPPOSITE: Raccoons have become so used to people that they're no longer afraid of them. They will go anywhere that people do. MICHELLE R. IACONIS

So when it comes to hunting, urban coyotes only have to look in one direction—at what they're chasing, not what's chasing them. That's not only a big relief; it's also a natural advantage. All their energy can go into hunting for food rather than becoming it. And because cities are so full of small animals—rats, mice, squirrels, voles and rabbits—there's lots of food for coyotes to hunt.

Also working to the coyote's advantage is that, just as they've become accustomed to living in cities, people have become accustomed to living with them. When they started showing up in many northern cities twenty or more years ago (in California they've been around forever), it was big news. What were they doing there? Were they dangerous? Did they eat children and pets? (Pets yes; children no.) Now, they're so firmly entrenched, we're used to them. We've had no choice because they wouldn't take no for an answer. When people rid an urban area of deer, it takes a long time for new deer to come back to that area. Somehow the message gets out within the deer community that it's booby-trapped. This isn't true of coyotes.

Amazing Animal Adaptation

There are almost as many stories about encounters with urban raccoons as there are raccoons themselves. Online you'll find all sorts of examples, such as the one about the college student who left a jug of milk near a screen door so it would get cold overnight, only to find a raccoon stuck in the door the next morning trying to drag the jug out. Or the one about the family of raccoons who ripped the pump out of a backyard pond and rearranged the rocks to their liking. Or the story about the two raccoons who had to be rescued from a Pepsi vending machine. The Seattle Aquarium lost a good number of the crustaceans in its crustacean exhibit to a hungry raccoon who refused to buy a ticket. If we build it, you can bet raccoons will come.

When people try to rid an urban area of coyotes, it's not long before new coyotes come along to fill the gap. So when a city or suburb becomes home to a population of coyotes, that's it, whether people like it or not.

There is another medium-sized, mid-level urban predator who's even more successful at city living. In fact, if one animal could lay claim to being the poster critter for all North American urban wildlife, it probably would be the raccoon, because they're almost everywhere. The reason, again, is that they're so adaptable. Even before there were cities, raccoons were animals whose living patterns changed with the seasons, the times and the landscapes. Whether a raccoon found itself in a forest (its preferred habitat), a prairie (not as desirable but okay) or a desert (worst of all), it would find a way to survive. As long as there was fresh water and something to eat, a raccoon would get by.

Well, a city is a whole lot more hospitable than a desert. Not only are raccoons relatively safe from predators in cities, but they're safe from hunger too. As nature's ultimate omnivore, a raccoon will eat almost anything—and almost anything is what cities are full of. Don't worry about those Dunkin' donuts you can't finish, because raccoons love 'em too. The same way they love ice cream, French fries, chicken strips, fish burgers, onion rings, potato chips and all the other pound-packing, heart-stopping junk North Americans shove in their faces every day. Cities are stuffed with junk like this, so cities are a banquet for raccoons.

But it's not just raccoons' free and easy diets that make them so adaptable. They'll also live just about anywhere. You won't catch a coyote building a den in someone's house.

Do raccoons wash their food?

No, it only looks as if they do. When raccoons bring a food item near water, they'll use their amazingly dexterous and humanlike forepaws to dunk it below the surface. But scientists now think they do this not to make sure that what they're about to eat is clean, but to excite the nerves in their paws and make them more sensitive. When their paws are sensitive, the raccoon can examine the food item more closely and figure out exactly what it is. Since raccoons don't have the best eyesight, they use their hands to help them "see" what their eyes can't.

✎ What makes skunk spray smell so bad?

Seven distinct chemical compounds combine to make what's called skunk "musk." Put them all together, and "WHOA!" The reason skunk musk is so offensive is that it smells of decay—of something rotting—which is a smell that tells us to STAY AWAY. For example, if you leave a piece of meat on the counter so long that it spoils, you'll know it's rotten and not fit to eat because of how it looks and, above all, smells. Skunk odor has the same effect.

In cities, domestic dogs are the most frequent victims of skunk spray. So what's the best way to wash them? For years, tomato juice was thought to be the answer, but it only masks the stink temporarily. Now more and more people put their faith in such things as vanilla extract, vinegar, orange juice, baking soda, certain kinds of laundry soap and even mouthwash. (They put cheap mouthwash in a spray bottle and shoot.) Unfortunately, there is no magic antidote except time. If you wait long enough, the smell will just wear away. But few people—and dogs—are that patient.

A raccoon won't think twice about it. As long as it's dry, private and safe, a mother raccoon will happily move in to have and look after her kits. No wonder raccoons are everywhere—or as good as. They've become as much a part of North American city life as traffic.

Another animal North American cities are now full of is the skunk. As a small animal not much bigger than a football (plus a tail), you might think skunks would be easy prey for predators. You'd be wrong. Thanks to their signature, *ahem*, perfume, predators have never put skunks high on their list of favorite prey. That's why skunks can run around in stark black-and-white stripes that advertise their existence. Thus protection from predators isn't the urban draw it is for other animals. No, the reason skunks can't get enough of city living is something more down-to-earth. Literally.

What skunks love about cities are city lawns and particularly the food—insects and insect larvae—found underneath them. North Americans also love lawns. We waste barrels of water keeping them dense and lush even in places where green grass was never meant to grow. (Think of all those thirsty golf courses in New Mexico, Arizona and Nevada.) The fact that we do, though, is great news for skunks, because when the soil lawns grow in is moist, insects and insect larvae—grubs—rise to the surface. And to a skunk there's nothing quite as satisfying as a nighttime feast of fat juicy grubs. That's why skunks think nothing of tearing up that carefully manicured front lawn your mom or dad worked so hard on last summer.

Unlike raccoons (and people), skunks don't eat junk food. They're a little pickier with their diets. But they do eat pet food, which we humans often leave lying around, and berries. So when we plant berry bushes next to our lush green lawns, it's skunk nirvana.

The last inadvertent kindness city folk show urban skunks is to till our soil. We're constantly turning over sod and soil to plant plants and build buildings. To an urban skunk, however, the purpose of all that earth moving is beside the point. What matters to them is that it's done at all. In the wild, skunks dig soil to build dens, but if a human is willing to do the job for them, they won't refuse the gesture. That's why you often see skunks living under houses, porches and decks.

Skunks, raccoons and coyotes tend to dominate our idea of urban wildlife because they're the urban animals we are likely to notice. They're the ones who make us stop and say "Hey!" and "Look!" and "Did you see that?" Yet when it comes to actual numbers of animals, they can't compare with another category of creature: the far less celebrated but far more numerous urban rodent. The rats, mice, voles, squirrels and shrews who scurry furtively through city lanes and, occasionally, city sewers, often under the cover of night, to avoid detection. Of course, when you consider how important rodents are in nature's **food chains**, it's no wonder there are so many. For many predators, rodents are dinner. Coyotes, foxes, raccoons, cougars and bobcats all eat them, as do many birds of prey, including hawks, eagles, owls and falcons (more about them in Chapter Four). So rodent parents have lots of young—up to a dozen at a time— to increase the odds of one or two surviving long enough to become parents themselves.

But while it is true that tens of thousands of rodents are eaten in cities every year, cities afford them a better chance of survival than they'd get in the wilderness. The reason is that there aren't as many predators in cities. Consequently, urban prey animals can multiply and multiply and multiply in a way they couldn't anywhere else. That's why when we talk about urban mammals,

TOP: Because squirrels find cities so hospitable, there's no telling where they'll appear. CATHERINE BELL

BOTTOM: Mice are almost as common in cities as rats because they eat much of the food humans throw away. WAYNE CAMPBELL

OPPOSITE: Urban squirrels can make their way into almost any nook or cranny. Then they have to be captured and set free. ORCA BOOK PUBLISHERS

What about flying mammals?

Gotham City was famous for being the home of Batman, but many other North American cities are home to bats too. When bats spread their wings, they may look like birds, but they're mammals. They have fur, not feathers, and their wings are made of skin stretched taut below their skeletal arms. Bats are nocturnal, which is why we never see them during the day. But when they do come out, they busy themselves by eating insects. In just one night a bat can eat his body weight in insects. That works out to about 500 mosquito-sized bugs every hour. So there's no reason to be afraid of bats, not when they do us such a big favor. In nature, bats hang out in caves during the day, but in cities they can use the attics of houses and buildings. The most common North American bat is the little brown bat, so named because of its nut-brown fur and small size. Its wingspan is only 8 inches (20 centimeters). More than fifty other bat species call the United States and Canada home, including the big brown bat, the evening bat and the eastern long-eared bat. Sadly, about 40 percent of all bat species are threatened with extinction. Even the little brown bat is in serious trouble in eastern North America because of the spread of a mysterious and deadly fungus.

what we're really talking about are rats, mice, voles, moles, shrews, squirrels and occasionally rabbits. We don't see them as readily as we do bears or deer because they're small and close to the ground, usually nocturnal and often hiding. (You'd hide too if you were on a coyote's breakfast menu!) But that doesn't mean they're not there. They are—in the tens upon tens of thousands.

That's also why, when we consider the ultimate urban animal, the animal we should consider first is the rat. Because wherever people and their great quantities of food go, rats follow. Have you ever heard the expression "like rats leaving a sinking ship"? We say it when people get out of somewhere in a hurry. Well, what do you think those rats were doing on the ship in the first place? Following people, that's what. Throughout history, rats have traveled all over the world on ships in the company of people, who have taken them everywhere. Few people would want to see a rat on a poster—leave that to the more photogenic raccoons. But when it comes to individual animal numbers, nothing compares to the urban rat. In fact, there are thought to be almost as many rats in the world as there are people.

Science has a name for animals who live closely with humans: **commensal**. Domestic dogs and cats are commensal; so are rats. The most numerous rat of all is the brown rat, named for its coarse brown fur. It's also called the sewer rat, common rat, wharf rat and Norway rat—the last because of a mistaken belief that the first brown rats to arrive in England in 1728 came aboard a Norwegian ship. Never mind that there were no rats in Norway at the time (there are now!). The only continent the brown rat doesn't live on is

Antarctica (just like people). And like people, rats are omnivores, meaning they'll eat almost anything, including much of what human beings throw out. So the more garbage there is lying around a house or a building or a city park, the more rats there'll be.

This is true of mice too. You may not realize mice are everywhere until your pet cat brings one home. Then you might wonder where it came from. But cities are full of mice because mice, like rats, also go where

people go. One of the most common is the house mouse. Voles, who look a lot like mice—except for a stouter body, and a slightly smaller head, eyes and ears—are also everywhere, especially in areas with green fields. And remember, North American cities are full of green places too.

And is there a city in the United States or Canada that isn't overrun with squirrels? Not likely. Most city squirrels are eastern gray squirrels, so named because they originated on the eastern side of North America. But now they live all over the west too. Squirrels do well in cities. In addition to nuts and seeds, which they eat in the wild, cities are full of bird feeders. And for squirrels a bird feeder is like an all-you-can-eat brunch at your favorite restaurant. Even though urban predators such as coyotes, foxes, owls and hawks hunt squirrels, there aren't enough predators to make a real dent in squirrel numbers. In other words, don't expect the squirrels scampering up the tree outside your window to disappear anytime soon.

Finally, in a few cities and towns on US plains you'll find black-tailed prairie dogs. That is no mean feat for this sneaker-sized rodent, because prairie dogs are among the most persecuted animals in North America. And that's saying a lot.

TOP: Skunks love lawns because of all the insects and insect larvae living under them. And because cities are so full of lawns, they're also full of skunks. THINKSTOCKPHOTOS.CA

BOTTTOM: Cities are full of rodents because cities are full of food that rodents eat. We don't see them easily because they live close to the ground and spend so much time hiding. But they're there. BLAIR COX

When the US West was still a wilderness, wolves, snakes and birds of prey kept their numbers in check. As with everything else in nature, it was a balance. But as more and more land was given over to more and more cattle, men with guns, traps and poison started to kill prairie dogs as well. And kill them they did—by the thousands. More than 90 percent of all the prairie dogs who once inhabited the US West are now gone.

Yet a few survived, somehow, to claim the odd patch of urban turf in cities like Denver and Boulder in Colorado, Albuquerque and Santa Fe in New Mexico, and Laramie in Wyoming, where they'll dig burrows wherever they can find a piece of ground not covered in concrete. Consequently you never know where one will turn up—next to a parking meter or outside a 7-Eleven. They're resilient that way. As long as they can find some seeds or plants to eat and a piece of earth where they aren't bothered by dogs, cars or construction, they survive long enough to breed and ensure, for the time being at least, that they don't disappear despite the best, cruelest and most ruthless efforts of humankind to eradicate them.

Scientists estimate that because of habitat loss, **climate change** and the destruction of various kinds of **ecosystems**, a quarter of the world's mammals are likely to disappear before the end of this century. They include animals as large as the polar bear and as small as the Christmas Island shrew. In 2006, the Yangtze River dolphin, a small long-nosed dolphin that Chinese legend says was born from a beautiful princess whose family tried to drown her for refusing to marry a man she didn't love, was declared extinct because of human activity. All these are animals, or mammals, who can't cope in a world brimming with people.

Yet there are exceptions. You met some of them here: the coyote, the skunk, the raccoon, the rat and others. There's another class of mammals, marine mammals, who live in the sea. Some of them have adjusted to city living too. You'll find out how in Chapter Two.

BOTTOM: The absence of wolves and, for the most part, cougars in North American cities means white-tailed deer can roam freely in them.
BARBARA SAUR

Chapter Two
Wet and Wild—Marine Mammals

When we think of urban wildlife, we rarely think of animals in water, because cities are built on land. But most cities are built *next* to water. Look at a map of the United States and Canada and see how many large cities are beside an ocean, a lake or a river. Almost any city of any appreciable size was built on a waterway because before there were cars and planes, ships and riverboats moved people and goods around. So critters who live in these waterways have inadvertently become city critters too.

Some of these critters are fish (more about them in Chapter Three). But some are only like fish in the sense that they, too, spend most or all of their lives in a marine environment. That's where the similarity ends. These critters are marine mammals because, unlike fish, they breathe in oxygen from the air, not the water, and their body temperatures are regulated internally, not by the outside environment. This means they're **warm-blooded**, like people. Seals, sea lions, dolphins, porpoises,

OPPOSITE: Because so many North American cities are situated by the sea, a number of marine mammals, including California sea lions, have become inadvertent city critters.
ANNE MCKINNELL
(HTTP://IMAGES.ANNEMCKINNELL.COM)

otters, whales and manatees are all marine mammals who live near or even in some of North America's biggest urban areas.

Look at that map of the United States and Canada again and notice how many big cities are on the ocean. Heading south down the Pacific coast, there's Vancouver, Seattle, San Francisco, Los Angeles, Long Beach and San Diego. Moving east along the Gulf, there's New Orleans and Tampa. And moving north up the Atlantic, there's Miami, Jacksonville, Baltimore, New York and Boston. In between are many smaller cities like Victoria, Santa Barbara, Galveston, Orange City, Cocoa Beach, Charleston, Bridgeport and Halifax. Each has its own distinct population of urban marine mammals living in the city or close by.

Have you ever seen a manatee? If you live in Florida or have visited there, perhaps you have. Maybe you were walking along a canal in Cocoa Beach or Jacksonville, enjoying the sunshine, when you saw something move. And there in the water staring back at you was a face as gentle as a cow's. Except attached to that face was a body as hefty as a bull's. That could be why people who love manatees, a very rare, very large and very docile animal that lives off the coast of South Florida, sometimes call them "sea cows." It can't be because they look like cows. If anything, manatees look like pale gray walruses with dewy eyes like a seal's and a paddle-shaped tail like a beaver's. They also have thick clear whiskers called *vibrisse* growing from their prominent snouts that make them look like professors.

Curiously, the manatee's closest relative isn't the walrus or the seal; it's the elephant, whom they resemble in size and color. The biggest manatees are over 10 feet (3 meters) long and weigh more than 2,000 pounds (900 kilograms). Perhaps, scientists say, millions of years ago the manatee's ancestor, an elephant-like creature, decided to leave the land and return to the water; no one really knows. Also like elephants, manatees eat only plants—heaps of them. Every day they fill their large stomachs with enough to equal a tenth or more of their body weight.

Finally, as with elephants, you have to be careful about getting too close to a manatee. Not that they're fierce; it's just that, being so heavy, they can throw their weight around. But despite their elephantine proportions, manatees—like every

ABOVE: It may be strange to think of a gray whale as an urban animal, but during the spring and fall they can be seen from urban coastlines, migrating between Alaska and California.
JESSIE HUGGINS/CASCADIA RESEARCH COLLECTIVE

🐋 Amazing Animal Adaptation

Like many other wild creatures in North America, manatees were never meant to be city critters. But in Florida they're now as much a part of some urban seascapes as raccoons, skunks and coyotes are of urban landscapes. And just like those animals, manatees have adapted to urban living in ways that both benefit and endanger them. If manatees need fresh water, they've learned to get it from the nearest leaky hose. They'll cadge people for food—even though feeding manatees is illegal. In places where it's legal for people to swim with manatees, they'll behave like pet dogs, rolling over on their backs and inviting people to scratch their bellies. They've even learned to pull the cords next to canal locks to ask lock keepers to let them through, as if they were captaining a boat or barge. (Given their size, in a way they are.) No wonder many Floridians think manatees are marvelous, and that the town of Orange City holds a manatee festival each January to celebrate its favorite city critter.

TOP: Harbor seals are among the most common visitors to urban shores. And with city harbors getting cleaner all the time, there are more of them than ever. CASCADIA RESEARCH COLLECTIVE

BOTTOM: Every year hundreds of harbor seals haul out onto Casa Beach in La Jolla, California, to give birth to new pups. And thousands of La Jolla residents watch them do it. US NATIONAL OCEANIC AND ATMOSPHERIC ADMINISTRATION

other kind of wild animal, including elephants—have much more to fear from us than we do from them. That's especially true in a city. The US Marine Mammal Protection Act forbids harming manatees or any marine mammal deliberately, but they can still get hurt, even killed, if they collide accidentally with a boat or Jet Ski. They can also get tangled in fishing line, choked by pollution and trapped in drainpipes and culverts. If a manatee gets stuck in a culvert, it can take an entire crew of highly trained professionals, including marine biologists and members of the fire department, to get him unstuck. Consequently, cities and their environs can be perilous places for manatees. They're also the main reasons Florida has only about 5,000 left.

The relationship between humans and any marine mammal is never trouble-free. Simply because of how many of us there are and how intrusive we can be, when it comes to the natural world we always do more harm than good. But this was true even before we got to be so plentiful. Think of how people in the eighteenth, nineteenth and early twentieth centuries hunted the world's great whales almost to extinction. Many species, including the largest animal ever to have lived, the blue whale, have yet to recover. So it is with most city marine mammals.

There are exceptions. The harbor seal, the bottlenose dolphin and the California sea lion all benefit from certain human-made structures in and around cities. They'll also take food from people and relate to them in an almost personal way. This is especially true of bottlenose dolphins, who live in the Gulf and the warmer parts of the Atlantic and Pacific. They'll even surf alongside human boarders on the California coast. So for them, city living isn't half bad.

This isn't true of most marine mammals. If they manage to survive in what scientists now call the "**urban ocean**," it's due

mainly to luck, tenacity and the willingness of some people to help them. Consider, for example, the North Atlantic right whale, or as some researchers call it, the urban whale, a gray-black leviathan who can grow to 60 feet (18 meters) in length and 140,000 pounds (64,000 kilograms) in weight. It may seem strange to think of a whale as being part of a city, but if you live in central or northeastern Florida (manatee land) or the small Massachusetts town of Provincetown on Cape Cod, there are times each year when you can pack a picnic and go watch one of the world's largest marine mammals (one of the largest animals who's ever lived) pass by.

Unfortunately right whales got their name for the wrong reasons. When whales were hunted commercially for their oil, the right whale was considered the correct or "right" whale to hunt because it boasted large amounts of blubber and was slow and easy to chase. Right whales also floated when they were dead, so whalers didn't have to worry about their carcasses sinking the way those of other species did. The consequence of this was that North Atlantic right whales almost disappeared

〜 What do whales eat?

Contrary to what you might think, many whales—huge as they are—eat mostly very tiny creatures. They just eat vast quantities of them. Gray whales, who live along the west coast of North America, eat almost 3,000 pounds (1,100 kilograms) of food a day, but that food is composed of tiny shrimp-like animals called amphipods who live on muddy ocean floors. They also eat herring eggs, crab larvae, tubeworms and small fishes. Every day a North Atlantic right whale will eat up to 4 million calories in zooplankton and copepods (tiny, almost microscopic animals that live near the surface of the sea and drift along with its currents). The average right whale is estimated to be 50 billion times bigger than the average copepod. Imagine if you were 50 billion times bigger than a French fry. You'd be bigger than a whale.

ABOVE: Northern right whales were hunted almost to extinction in the last two hundred years. Now the few who are left have to navigate through the busy shipping lanes that feed into eastern coastal cities. KATIE JACKSON, FLORIDA FISH AND WILDLIFE COMMISSION, NOAA FISHERIES, TAKEN UNDER PERMIT #594-1759

from the sea and remain critically endangered today. There are no more than 450 or so in the whole world.

An international ban on commercial whaling has made killing right whales illegal, but they continue to die accidentally in collisions with ships. Nevertheless, enough survive in the Atlantic to be seen from urban areas off the east coast of Florida from December to March, when females give birth to calves, and briefly in spring from Provincetown, Massachusetts, when they migrate north to the Canadian ocean. This means even casual observers can help keep track of them and so lessen the chance of their swimming afoul of a freighter. When urban whale watchers report the whereabouts of right whales to the Coast Guard, the latter can tell ships to avoid them. With the help of such watchers, perhaps the right whale population won't decline any more.

When scientists speak of the urban ocean, they mean not just the ocean at the city's edge, but also the water a few miles (or several kilometers) off its coast. This is the ocean of ships and shipping traffic converging into lanes that head into ports. This is also the ocean that's so treacherous to marine mammals. If you doubt that, consider the case of the southern right whale, the North Atlantic right whale's southern-hemisphere cousin. By 1935, the year commercial whaling ended, the southern right whale also was hunted almost to extinction. Yet today there are more than 10,000 in the world compared to only 450 northern whales. Why? Because southern whales live in a much less urban ocean, so they're not exposed to as many dangers. Who knows how many North Atlantic right whales there would be today if they didn't have to traverse the busy shipping highways feeding into New York, Boston and Halifax?

Nevertheless, even in an ocean as busy as that next to California, the gray whale has made a stunning comeback. There are now thought to be more than 20,000 of these 50-foot (15-meter), 80,000-pound (36,000-kilogram) giants in the eastern Pacific. From Point Loma, a hilly, prosperous and fairly well-populated peninsula within Greater San Diego, you can see gray whales as they make their way to and from their Baja breeding grounds from mid-December to March. Just stand in the park overlooking the coast, and there they'll be in all their seagoing splendor, despite the presence of America's ninth-largest city and one of its biggest naval bases only a few miles away. What effect that naval base has on the whales is still being studied. Whales and other marine mammals rely on sonar to figure out where they are and how to move forward, so ship noise can disrupt those signals and affect their movements. This may be true of California's grays, too, but so far it doesn't appear to have had a discernible impact.

When it comes to truly urban whales, however, few compare to the single young migrating gray who caused a citywide commotion in Vancouver in the late spring of 2010 when he swam into False Creek, an urban inlet bordered by twenty-story apartments. People couldn't believe their eyes. Even the police turned out to see him. What was a whale that size (35 feet or 10.6 meters) doing in the middle of the city in the middle of the day? The answer, scientists reckon, is that he either lost his way or was searching for food along the shallow bottom (not a good idea as it's polluted). Prior to his stunning appearance, this was an unheard-of event in Vancouver, which goes to show how unpredictable city critters can be. We never know where they're going to turn up next.

How smart are whales and dolphins?

People often make the mistake of using human intelligence as a barometer for other animals' cleverness. Doing this is a disservice to those animals because they've evolved differently from humans to live in different ways. So what's smart for a person may be stupid for a chicken or a goat. Nevertheless, scientists now believe that when you consider brain size, levels of self-awareness, sociability and behavioral complexity, whales and dolphins probably score somewhere between chimpanzees and humans. This has prompted some scientists to refer to them as "brainiacs beneath the waves."

ABOVE: The notion of an urban whale is becoming more and more common thanks to all the urban waterways that feed US and Canadian coastal cities. JESSIE HUGGINS/CASCADIA RESEARCH COLLECTIVE

ABOVE: Bottlenose dolphins are among the most gregarious of marine mammals. They show up in ports throughout the southern United States, including Florida and California. B. PRITCHETT

Farther south, a marine mammal well known to coastal communities from Florida through Louisiana, Georgia and Texas to California is that previously mentioned and highly gregarious bottlenose dolphin. You can even see them off the coast of Los Angeles, the second-largest city in the United States and home to its busiest port. Bottlenose dolphins are about 6 to 8 feet (2 to 2.5 meters) long, blue-gray along their backs and white on their tummies. They have a long snout, or "bottle nose" (hence their name), a blowhole on top of their heads and a turned-up mouth that makes them look as if they're perpetually smiling. But the smile can be a joker's grin. In fact, male bottlenose dolphins can be very aggressive and will fight each other for top spot in a pod (a group of dolphins). They're also very smart and easy to train, which is why, to the dismay of dolphin lovers, they're often captured for use in marine shows.

Out at sea, though, swimming freely in the harbors of such cities as Miami, San Diego, Galveston and Tampa, they appear to be happy in the company of people. Or if not happy, at least used to it. As with manatees and other kinds of urban critters, it's wrong—and illegal—to feed bottlenose dolphins because it makes them dependent on people for food. But sometimes people feed them accidentally. If a fisherman catches a fish the law says is too small to keep, he has to throw it back. Well, guess who'll

🐋 Amazing Animal Adaptation

Have you ever heard the expression "like shooting fish in a barrel"? Bottlenose dolphins have adapted a method of fishing that is the dolphin equivalent. If humans build a wall along a harbor as a foundation for some sort of structure, dolphins are smart enough to drive the fish directly into the wall so the fish can't escape. They do the same with human-made canals. They chase the fish to the point where the canal ends. Then it's dolphin dinnertime. Bottlenose dolphins also will hitch rides on the bow waves of large ships. That way they don't have to use their own energy to travel. Instead, like first-class passengers on an ocean liner, they rely on the ship. Or maybe they do it for fun. Only they know for sure.

eat that fish when he does. Same thing if he catches the wrong kind of fish. In a dolphin's eyes, there's no such thing, so that's more dolphin dinner.

Returning to southwestern British Columbia and the US Pacific Northwest, it's rare to see urban whales or dolphins, that gobsmacking case of the Vancouver gray whale aside. (Though you can see grays off the coast of Everett, a small city north of Seattle.) If you travel by ferry from either the US or Canadian mainland to Vancouver Island, you might be lucky enough to see killer whales, or orcas, en route. There are three orca pods, totaling about 88 animals, who frequent the Strait of Juan de Fuca. But close as these waters are to Seattle and Vancouver, it's unusual for an orca to swim into either city. Which is why the sight of six of them making their way up Burrard Inlet, one of Vancouver's principal waterways and the site of its main harbor, caused such a stir in spring 2010. Researchers at the Vancouver Aquarium were agog. How could such a thing happen? No one knows for sure. Yet there they were, six splendid oceangoing reminders that when it comes to nature and her mysteries, almost nothing is certain except uncertainty.

Pacific white-sided dolphins and harbor porpoises are smaller marine mammals who also live in that wet, fairly chilly part of the world. They, like orcas, navigate the urban ocean bordering Seattle and Vancouver, but they, too, rarely swim near those cities. Again, that is, until recently. On the very day after the gray whale turned up in False Creek in 2010, a pod of Pacific white-sided dolphins went herring fishing off the coast of West Vancouver, a posh Vancouver suburb. The same thing happened a year later, except even more dolphins showed up. What changed? Ocean currents and the food supply, scientists reckon, but they need to do more research to be sure.

What's the difference between a dolphin and a porpoise?

Porpoises are smaller than dolphins. They never grow more than 7 feet (2.3 meters) long, whereas dolphins can grow to 10 feet (3 meters) long. Porpoises have small round heads and no beaks. Most dolphins have a long nose or snout. Killer whales, who belong to the dolphin family, are an exception. They also have a round face and no beak. And while a porpoise's dorsal fin is triangle-shaped, a dolphin's dorsal fin is shaped like an ocean wave. Dolphins and porpoises also behave differently. Most porpoises are very shy and fearful of people, but dolphins will go up to boats and surfers with little hesitation. Dolphins also live longer—up to fifty years compared to only about fifteen for a porpoise.

ABOVE: The manatee's closest living relative is the elephant. Millions of years ago, elephantlike creatures may have moved into the sea, where they lost their legs and developed the ability to swim. PATRICK M. ROSE/ SAVETHEMANATEE.ORG

What's the difference between a seal and a sea lion?

Seals have ear holes and no ear flaps. Sea lions have ear flaps like a dog's. Seals always swim with their hind flippers, which face backward and are furred. Sea lions swim with their front flippers and are able to turn their hind flippers forward. Amazingly for a marine mammal, sea lions can also walk when they haul themselves on land. They use all four of their flippers as if they were feet. Seals move more like sacks of laundry being dragged across a floor. Seal moms have two teats for their pups, and sea lion moms have four. And whereas seals can swim in both marine and fresh-water environments, sea lions are only ever found in the ocean.

ABOVE: Occasionally harbor seals will take food from people and relate to them in an almost human way. JOHN CALAMBOKIDIS/CASCADIA RESEARCH COLLECTIVE

Whatever the reason, it was one more eyepopper from Mother Nature.

In contrast, a longtime and almost daily visitor to both Seattle's and Vancouver's harbors—as well as harbors along both American coasts—is the harbor seal, a cute, round-faced windsock of a marine mammal with big whiskers, dark fur and soulful eyes. If you're walking along the seafront and see what looks like a bowling ball pop out of the water, chances are it's the head of a harbor seal, especially if the bowling ball turns out to have a sleek curvy body, flippers and a stubby tail.

In Seattle, not far from the Space Needle, there's a fish ladder rising from Elliott Bay to Lake Washington. In the fall, when the returning salmon swim up the ladder, hungry harbor seals turn up too, to greet and eat them. The fish ladder, which was built to facilitate an ancient salmon run in what is now a city of more than 600,000 people, has made life a little easier for the harbor seal and turned it into a bona fide city critter.

In Newport, Oregon, a picturesque port town 114 miles (184 kilometers) west of Portland, the seal's pickings are still richer. There are three fish-processing plants in Newport (such plants used to exist up and down the west coast until fish populations declined from **overfishing**), and leftovers from them are gravy to a harbor seal.

Even in New York City, one of America's busiest ports, you can now see harbor seals staring up at the Statue of Liberty. At least they look as if they are. This is due to the fact that New York harbor, like most city harbors, is cleaner than it used to be. A cleaner harbor is a more hospitable harbor, and that's good news not just for seals, but all marine mammals.

In La Jolla, just north of San Diego, harbor seals are such a part of the city that they've become a tourist attraction. On a well-protected half moon of sand called Casa Beach, female harbor seals routinely give birth to seal pups in full view of hundreds of people. It's not that the seals want the people there or that the people do something to help them—if anything, they do the opposite. Casa Beach is simply where the seals have decided to have their pups. It just happens to be on the edge of a busy big-city suburb. And if the seals are bothered by having so many prying eyes watching their every intimate move, they don't show it. During pup season, from December 15 to May 15, the beach is off-limits to people. Thanks to pressure put on city authorities by some La Jolla residents, the beach is for seals and seals alone. People may gather on a nearby seawall to watch them, but that's all. During those five months, up to 200 seals give birth to as many as 45 pups, all within about 6 feet (1.8 meters) of what can be a gallery of hundreds of staring, gawking, wondering human eyes. Not surprisingly, closing the beach has caused conflict between people who want to use it year-round and people who put the seals' needs first, but so far the seals have won the day.

During the summer, however, people and seals are allowed to mix freely. If you swim off Casa Beach between June and November, you're almost guaranteed to run—or swim—into a harbor seal. People who protect the seals believe this kind

ABOVE: The sea lions who haul out onto San Francisco's Pier 39 are arguably the most urban marine mammals in the world. An estimated 14 million people visit Pier 39 each year, making it the twelfth most popular tourist attraction on Earth. PIER 39, SAN FRANCISCO

of contact stresses them, so they advise against it. Yet during an average month, lifeguards posted at Casa Beach say about 116,000 people will come by to look at the seals and occasionally swim with them, making them among the most urbanized marine mammals on the continent—maybe in the world.

Rivals for this title are the 900 or so California sea lions who converge on Pier 39 in the heart of San Francisco's downtown waterfront. Unlike Casa Beach, Pier 39, a 300-berth marina, isn't a beach. It's a dock and, like all docks, was built as a place for people to tie up their boats. But that hasn't stopped the sea lions from taking over. In 1990, shortly after the terrifying 1989 Loma Prieta earthquake that shook San Francisco to its core, California sea lions—1,000-pound (450-kilogram) males and smaller 350-pound (158-kilogram) females—began hauling themselves out of the water and onto the pier. Whether the earthquake was responsible for this behavior isn't known. What is known is that after the earthquake the fish supply in the harbor changed,

and the seals took advantage. When their fishing was done, they needed a place to rest, and Pier 39 fit the bill.

Hauling out is the term biologists give the period when seals and sea lions haul themselves onto dry land to rest. Normally they haul out onto rocks or beaches, but if humans choose to make a pier available to them in one of the world's most celebrated city harbors, they aren't about to say no. At first the Pier 39 sea lions numbered about 50, but with lots of herring in the harbor, ample dock space and a sheltered environment far away from the churning swells of the Pacific, more arrived. Then more and more, until about 900 of the honking, snuffling, snorting sea mammals crowded the dock like so many socks in a drawer.

Most of them leave San Francisco over the summer. They swim south to the Channel Islands off Santa Barbara and Los Angeles to breed. But some hang around all year, earning the nickname "Sea Lebrities" from staff at a nearby marine mammal center. Each weekend, weather permitting, tour guides introduce visitors to the sea lions and explain their behavior.

And when that's done, you can always have a drink and dinner at—where else?—the Pier 39 Sea Lion Café.

Sea lions, like harbor seals, live up and down the west coast of the United States and Canada, and they, like Pier 39's "Sea Lebrities," make use of human-made structures too. In Victoria, the capital of British Columbia on the southernmost tip of Vancouver Island, there's a long narrow breakwater at Ogden Point, the place where cruise ships tie up on their way to Alaska. And just as on Pier 39, crowds of dark and golden brown sea lions, some as dense and heavy as punching bags, will loll around on the concrete foundations completely indifferent to the

ABOVE: These California sea lions decided to take a break from navigating the waters of Puget Sound to admire the Seattle skyline. PAT GEARIN/ NOAA, NATIONAL MARINE MAMMAL LABORATORY

What's the difference between a sea otter and a river otter?

Sea otters are found only in the ocean and rarely come on land, whereas river otters swim in rivers, streams and the sea. They also get around very well on land. Sea otter tails are shorter than a river otter's, and they have paddle-shaped hind feet, not webbed feet. Sea otters spend a lot of time floating on their backs. They rest, groom and feed in this position. River otters never do. And sea otters travel in large groups, whereas river otters are mainly solitary.

ABOVE: Pacific white-sided dolphins navigate the chilly ocean waters off such coastal cities as Vancouver and Seattle. Traditionally they've never gone near those cities, but lately that's begun to change. LANCE BARRETT-LENNARD/ VANCOUVER AQUARIUM

hordes of people who turn up to watch them. That's the upside of city living. The downside is that they risk being struck and even killed by a cruise ship entering or leaving the harbor.

Last, and in a way least because they don't spend their whole lives in the ocean, are river otters. There are sea otters, too, but they rarely visit cities. If you're lucky, you might see a group near Victoria now and then, and more if you visit Alaska, where there are thousands. In California a few might pop up near Monterey among the seals, sea lions and brown pelicans. But you're much more likely to see a river otter. As befits their name, river otters live on or near rivers, which is why they can also be found in such cities as Minneapolis and St. Paul, Minnesota. Since rivers empty into the sea, it follows that river otters live along seafronts too. In fact, whenever river otters are spotted near ocean cities like Bellingham, Newport or Portland, Maine, people tend to assume they're sea otters.

River otters are the clowns of the sea—its acrobats. They wrestle like children, belly flop off rocks, turn somersaults and corkscrews, and slide down almost any slippery slope for the sheer joy of it. An animal that agile and mischievous is a treat to watch, but it takes patience, given that river otters can hold their breath up to four minutes. This allows them to fish underwater, but it also may leave you wondering where that incredibly cute, dark-eyed, mustachioed sea monkey has gone. If you're patient, though, chances are you'll get to see it again, because like their landlubber cousins, the urban skunk, river otters have little fear of humans. They go where they want, and if humans are there too, so what.

In Seattle, river otters climb the same Elliott Bay fish ladder seals do to hunt salmon. In other places they'll shadow clam diggers in hopes of getting their paws on what the diggers drop. And just like raccoons and squirrels who nest in attics or basements of city houses, river otters will build dens in the cellars and alcoves of waterfront homes. They'll even rip fiberglass insulation out of walls to use as nesting material. And if you can't see them, you'll still know they're there from their distinctive otter "aroma" of fish and feces.

But everything has its price, including such brazen nonchalance. River otters won't think twice about crossing roads…and guess how that ends.

What's extraordinary about river otters is that they straddle both the wet and the dry worlds—just as we do. But by doing so, they illustrate how difficult it is to say where an urban area begins and ends. When a city is on an ocean or a large lake, does it cease to exist where the land ceases to exist? More and more scientists who study marine mammals and other sea creatures say no. Not when that urban ocean—the ocean that supports the activities of so many people—is so near.

Freighters travel that ocean. So do oil tankers, cruise ships, fishing boats and pleasure craft— everything from rowboats to million-dollar yachts. They're all part of urban living, and, for marine mammals, a challenging fact of life. When the Deepwater Horizon, a British Petroleum oil rig, blew up in the Gulf of Mexico in 2010, it caused the worst environmental disaster in US history. Marine life died not just where it exploded, but all along the Gulf coast too. Yet similar rigs continue to drill oil from Newfoundland to Mexico in an urban ocean full of marine mammals.

Some of them, as this chapter has explained, have learned to live in that urban ocean—or at least tried to. Like so many other kinds of wildlife in today's modern world, they've had no choice.

ABOVE: River otters won't think twice about building dens in the basements of riverfront houses. The fact that they're so cute makes it harder to get angry with them. C.J. CASSON/ SEATTLE AQUARIUM

Chapter Three

Waterworld—Fish and Other Aquatic Creatures

I f you live in a city by the sea—and millions of North Americans do—you'll know the sea has a big effect on that city. Wind and weather blow in from it. Movement is limited by it. If you want to cross it, you have to use a plane or a boat. The sea shapes cities, too, because once a city reaches its edge, it can't spread farther in that direction.

Cities on large lakes are affected the same way—think of Chicago on Lake Michigan, Toronto on Lake Ontario and Detroit on Lake St. Clair. Cities on rivers aren't contained by those rivers—there are bridges—but their landscape is still affected by them. Think of Montreal on the St. Lawrence, Calgary on the Bow and Pittsburgh on the Ohio, the Allegheny and the Monongahela. The latter two rivers flow into the first, and downtown Pittsburgh is located at the point where all three rivers meet. The US capital, Washington, DC, sits on the Potomac River. Canada's capital, Ottawa, is on the Ottawa River. These ribbons of water help define these cities in the same way the sea defines coastal cities.

OPPOSITE: As long as they're rocky, urban shorelines can host any number of interesting and colorful marine species, including these ocher sea stars. For reasons scientists don't understand, ocher sea stars sometimes turn purple.
VINCENT LOUIS/DREAMSTIME.COM

⚹ How polluted is the ocean?

No one can say for sure, but recent research shows that even sperm whales, who can dive up to 9,800 feet (3,000 meters) deep, contain shockingly high levels of toxic metals in their tissue, suggesting that human-made poisons are reaching even the farthest corners of the ocean. Samples of whale tissue studied contained high levels of cadmium, aluminum, chromium, lead, silver, mercury and titanium. Various chemical poisons have also been found in the skin of Antarctic penguins, even though they don't live anywhere near people or industry.

So, as the last chapter suggested, it makes sense when we talk about city critters to talk about water critters too. Chapter Two discussed marine mammals, those who live mostly in the sea, but this one will discuss other kinds of aquatic creatures, both marine and freshwater—animals like crabs, clams, mussels and fish. Yes, fish, and not just in aquariums. In urban rivers throughout North America, wild fish continue to live and breed despite a long history of pollution.

This wasn't always so. In 1969 the Cuyahoga River in Cleveland, Ohio, became a national symbol of just how dirty urban waterways could be when it caught fire after some oil-soaked debris suddenly ignited. The fire burned for two hours and was a terrible "black eye" to the city, known then for its heavily polluting industries. Almost immediately Cleveland became an emblem of progress gone wrong—and it was an image that stuck.

But Mother Nature is resilient. If we lend her a helping hand by getting rid of water-borne pollutants, fish and other aquatic life return. Cleveland learned that in the 1970s and '80s when city officials undertook a major cleanup of the Cuyahoga, described then as "a sewer running through the heart of the city." Today it's a river where walleye, bass, northern pike and other aquatic creatures swim, feed and hunt in a way that would have been impossible forty years ago.

A similar phenomenon has taken place in the Pacific Northwest. In cities like Vancouver, Bellingham, Seattle and Olympia there are now creeks and streams where five species of Pacific salmon swim. In autumn, adult salmon swim upstream to spawn and die. The following spring, the eggs they laid and fertilized hatch to produce fry that swim downstream to the ocean.

What's remarkable is that they do this in full view of an urban skyline. But long before there were cities on the Pacific, there was a temperate rainforest where salmon were king. Many streams that ran through that forest were dammed to make way for cities. Now, thanks to the recent efforts of conservationists and governments, they've been reopened to salmon and other fish. As a result, the Pacific salmon has become one more urban critter.

This is also true of creatures living along city seashores. It may seem strange to classify mussels, oysters, shrimp and crab as urban wildlife, but they are in the sense of where they live. If you call a port city like Boston, Seattle, Halifax or San Francisco home, you'll know that if you travel down to the docks and look over the edge at the pilings, they'll be carpeted with sea life—a dense and variegated rug of seaweed, barnacles, mussels and other growth. Whoever built those docks didn't do so with the idea of providing habitat for sea life; it just worked out that way.

Needless to say, the creatures who cling to those dock pilings don't know they were built by humans. Nor do they care. It's just that mussels, barnacles and periwinkles (a type of sea snail commonly found along the New England coast) need something to grab hold of to survive. In the wild they cement themselves to rocks, then filter the water that passes over those rocks for food. In a city, when they encounter rocklike structures like pilings, drainpipes or even ships' hulls, they cling to them in the same way. And in doing so, they become city critters.

This is especially true in Seattle, where there's very little natural rocky shore; it's mostly pebbly beach. But thanks to all the concrete structures built along Elliott Bay and other Puget Sound waterfronts, it's a place where coastal creatures thrive. In Vancouver, the foundation of the city's new harborfront convention center was built purposely to foster marine life.

ABOVE: We may not think of barnacles, crabs and sea snails as urban wildlife, but as long as a city has a rocky shoreline, they become *de facto* city dwellers. CHRISTOPHER HARLEY

OPPOSITE TOP: The Santa Monica Pier is one of the Los Angeles area's premier tourist attractions. It's also home to many varieties of marine life that cling to its undersides and pilings. CINDY BENDAT/SANTA MONICA PIER

OPPOSITE BOTTOM: Sea anemones look more like plants than animals, but they're among the critters found in the lowest level of the intertidal zone. LAURA COX

In California, there are almost twenty piers extending into the Pacific, all of them artificial—and accidental—hosts to a tapestry of sea life. Similar piers exist in Florida, Maine, Maryland, New Jersey, New York, Virginia and Texas too.

The variety of marine creatures near a city's shore isn't as great as it is farther out, but it's still impressive. When it comes to fish, Pacific coast cities are hosts not just to salmon, but also herring and Pacific sand lance, a finger-long silver fish shaped like a knife blade. On the world-famous Santa Monica Pier in Greater Los Angeles (built in 1909 as a support for sewer pipes), fishermen have been known to catch perch, mackerel, white sea bass, leopard and tiger sharks, and sting rays—all within the sound of busy restaurants, stores and even an amusement park.

Over on the Atlantic, you're likely to see schools of American shad, a largish (16 to 24 inches or 40 to 60 centimeters long) silvery brown fish that, like salmon, swims in from the sea and lays its eggs in rivers. On the Atlantic City Boardwalk, arguably the most celebrated pier in North America, you might see striped bass, kingfish and flounder. The biggest striped bass ever caught (78 pounds or 35 kilograms) was hooked in 1982 from the Vermont Avenue jetty, famous as a property on the original Monopoly game board.

★ Amazing Animal Adaptation

Most Seattle residents are probably unaware that a colony of sixgill sharks, the third-largest predatory shark in the world, is breeding just 50 feet (15 meters) below the city's aquarium. What's remarkable about this is that sixgill sharks, which can grow to be 15 feet (almost 5 meters) long and have a mouthful of sharp teeth, normally live 1,000 feet (305 meters) below the ocean's surface. But not in Seattle, where, for reasons still known only by the sharks, they've decided to move up in the world (so to speak) to a depth previously unheard of. However, it may be a good thing for them, because sixgill sharks, like so many shark species around the world, are under terrific threat. At least this way they're living under the constantly concerned eyes of a team of marine scientists trying to understand why they moved so near the surface and how best to save them everywhere.

When it comes to shore life, what you'll find on city waterfronts won't vary much from coast to coast to coast. The variety of life on the Pacific is slightly richer than on the Atlantic or Gulf coasts because the ice covering the eastern half of the continent during the last ice age was thicker than in the west. So a greater variety of sea life survived in the west.

Regardless of where you live, however, the place to find shore life is in what biologists call the **intertidal zone**, the stretch of shore between the highest and lowest tide points. This zone is only visible when the tide is out, but it's easy to spot because it never dries out completely. In a way it looks like a really thick bathtub ring stretching from one end of the shore to the other. You can also see it on dock pilings, where it looks as if the color of the piling has been darkened.

How wide the intertidal zone is depends on how high the tide rises, and that depends on a variety of factors such as the time of year, where the sun and moon are in the sky (their gravitational pull makes tides happen) and where the stretch of coast is located (the Bay of Fundy, between New Brunswick and Nova Scotia, has one of the highest tides in the world at 55.1 feet or 16.8 meters). But whatever its size, creatures in the intertidal zone are unique among marine life—and city critters—in that they live in saltwater for part of the day and dry, sometimes hot, air for the other part. That makes them very hardy creatures indeed.

The top layer of the intertidal zone, called the splash zone because it only gets wet when waves splash it, has little life in it beyond a few lichens and bacteria. This is because it's dry most of the time and vulnerable to predators like seabirds. But as you move down the zone, plants such as rockweed and sea lettuce appear. Rockweed, as its name suggests, is a kind of seaweed (full of nutrients but hard to chew), while sea lettuce is a type of green algae that looks remarkably like salad lettuce.

★ **What are the busiest ports in the United States and Canada?**

Measured according to the amount of container traffic they handle each year, the ten busiest ports in the United States and Canada are (in order) Los Angeles, Long Beach, New York/New Jersey, Vancouver, Montreal, Savannah, Oakland, Norfolk/Virginia Beach, Seattle and Tacoma.

ABOVE: In the wilderness, mussels cling to rocks to survive. In a city, concrete or wooden pilings will do. LAURA COX

OPPOSITE TOP: As long as a city has pilings and piers in it, any number of different kinds of marine life will cling to them. COLIN MILLS

OPPOSITE BOTTOM: You have to be patient to see a sea star because they live at the lowest level of the intertidal zone, meaning the tide has to be far out before they're visible. LAURA COX

TOP: Look closely at certain kinds of marine life that grow along urban shorelines, and they can resemble flowers—even cauliflowers.
CHRISTOPHER HARLEY

BOTTOM: Numerous sea star species live along urban shores, so identifying them correctly can take time. This one is a leather sea star. LAURA COX

Except that when it dies, it stinks of rotten eggs. The smell is so strong that if you walk along a seafront with sea lettuce, you may want to hold your nose. If you live in Boston, for example, you'll know that parts of the harbor can be choked with it in summer. But as with everything in nature, it has its purpose. The rotten-egg smell is due to sulfur, which is emitted when organic material rots. And even though it may cause us to gag, it provides food for lots of different marine organisms.

Living among this intertidal plant life are various species of barnacles and periwinkles, small squishy creatures who live most of their lives encased in hard shells. These creatures—particularly the barnacles—are the bane of city sailors because they don't distinguish between rocks and boats when they look for surfaces to cling to. They'll happily stick to either. So if you're a boat owner, you'll know that scraping the barnacles that accumulated on your hull over winter can be a backbreaking rite of spring. There are also shore crabs in this part of the zone. On the beach, if you see crabs the size of your thumb scurrying every which way when you overturn a rock, what you're seeing are shore crabs—named for where they live. They're probably the first urban marine creatures many city residents notice.

Midway along the intertidal zone, which is underwater for more hours than the layers above it, you'll find oysters, mussels, sea worms and hermit crabs, which are especially common on Atlantic shores. Hermit crabs are interesting because, unlike other crabs, they don't have hard shells to protect them. Instead they wear shells borrowed from snails. But because snail shells come in all sorts of shapes and sizes, a hermit crab never knows what kind of shell it's going to get. Like women trying on hats in a store, one crab might wear a tall skinny shell while another will wear a squat round one.

At the lowest level of the intertidal zone—that is, at the level underwater the longest—you'll find more hermit crabs, red rock crabs (which are about the size of your hand), sea anemones (they look more like plants than animals) and dog whelks, a small carnivorous sea snail with a tongue like a chainsaw blade that the whelk uses to drill through limpet shells and suck out the soft mucous animal inside. You also may find various sea stars. One of the most common is the ocher sea star. If you live in a city like Santa Barbara or San Diego on the open ocean, that's exactly what you'll see: an ocher-colored or vaguely orange- or brown-colored animal with five arms stretched out in five different directions. But if you live in a city like Seattle or Vancouver that's shielded from the ocean (Vancouver by Vancouver Island and Seattle by the Olympic Peninsula), the ocher sea star turns deep purple. No one knows why.

Whether you get to see any of these animals depends on the height of the tide and also on whether the shore you're standing on is rocky, as it's only rocky shores that support life of this kind. Sandy beaches don't have a lot of marine life on them. There might be the odd sea turtle if you live along the Gulf, or a sand dollar if you live anywhere else. (Sand dollars are flat round sea creatures related to the sea star, but with a hard round exterior skeleton the size of a cookie.) Because animals can't attach themselves to sand, they aren't safe on beaches, so they don't live on them. Also, if we can see prey animals on the sand, so can predators. That's why animals like clams and snails always hide below the sand.

What you do see along city beaches are clamshell pieces. They look like crockery pieces, only smaller and finer. They're there because predators toss them aside when they've finished eating the mucous animals inside. Birds either break open the shells with their beaks or shatter them on rocks. So if you want to find a whole clam inside a whole clamshell, you'll have to use a shovel—and a little elbow grease.

A third kind of marine environment that exists on the east coast of North America from New Brunswick south, along the Gulf coast to Texas and in a few spots along the Pacific, is the **salt marsh**. Salt marshes are tidal wetlands less salty than the ocean—what scientists call "brackish"—present in bays, lagoons and at the mouths of creeks and rivers. Tall grasses and other non-woody plants grow in them, and like the urban rocky shore, they're home to a wide variety of marine life, including blue, fiddler and horseshoe crabs, the grass shrimp,

ABOVE: Goldfish who began their lives as pets sometimes end up as urban fish when their owners pitch them into nearby streams and rivers. © SHEDD AQUARIUM/BRENNA HERNANDEZ

BELOW: Many of America's great cities were built along salt marshes, and some of those marshes continue to survive today, including this one in Brooklyn. NEW YORK CITY URBAN PARK RANGERS

various snails, worms, clams and ribbed mussels, a kind of mussel that anchors itself to the marsh soil and keeps it from eroding.

However, like many other North American wild places, salt marshes have become endangered because cities were built on them. When European immigrants began arriving in the New World four hundred years ago, they often settled in salt marshes because the soil was good for farming and the nearby river made drinking, irrigation and transport easy. A number of America's great coastal cities, including New York, Boston and Baltimore, were all built on salt marshes, and marshes still exist in and around some of them. On the northern tip of New York, in a place called Inwood Hill Park, there are traces of the original salt marsh that once lined three sides of Manhattan. In nearby Brooklyn (named after the Dutch word for "broken land") is the 400-acre (162-hectare) Salt Marsh Nature Center. You can see the Empire State Building from the southern tip of it. In Queens and the Bronx there are several small salt marshes too.

Chesapeake Bay, the largest estuary in the United States, is also home to many salt marshes and much urban development, including the cities of Baltimore and, farther inland, Washington, DC. Seventy-five miles from Baltimore and eighty-five (121 and 137 kilometers, respectively) from Washington is the Blackwater Wildlife Refuge, a 25,000-acre (10,117-hectare) salt marsh referred to as "the Everglades of the north" because it represents one-third of all existing wetlands in the state of Maryland. In Massachusetts, about 35 miles (56 kilometers) north-east of Boston is the 17,000-acre (6,880-hectare) Great Salt Marsh, which extends all the way to the New Hampshire border. Farther south in South Carolina, the elegant city of Charleston is surrounded by salt marshes. Visitors can take ecotours of them, where they'll see not just small marine critters, but dolphins, birds and alligators too. And it was the salt marshes in Louisiana—some of them near New Orleans—and elsewhere along the Gulf that suffered so terribly after the Deepwater Horizon oil rig exploded in 2010. Who knows how long it will take them to recover—if ever?

Philadelphia, one of America's oldest cities, was also built on a marsh. In 1682, settlers from the Old World established the city where the Delaware and Schuylkill Rivers meet. But unlike New York, Philadelphia was built on a freshwater tidal marsh, meaning it's less salty than a salt marsh. Two hundred acres (81 hectares) of that marsh remain in the form of the John Heinz National Wildlife Refuge near the city's airport. More than 300 bird species use this refuge as a resting stop where they feed on crayfish, freshwater mussels and other aquatic life. A similar, though much bigger (2,277-acre or 921-hectare) refuge, named the Elizabeth Hartwell Mason Neck Wildlife Refuge, exists on the Potomac River 18 miles (29 kilometers) south of Washington, DC. This refuge, the largest freshwater marsh in northern Virginia, is home to the largest great blue heron rookery in the US Mid-Atlantic region. It also hosts

ABOVE: Much of New York City was built on a salt marsh. Here's another one at the Jamaica Bay Wildlife Refuge in Queens. NEW YORK CITY URBAN PARK RANGERS

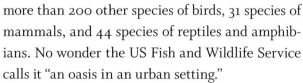

★ What are America's ten most endangered rivers?

As determined by the conservation group American Rivers, they are the Upper Delaware in Pennsylvania and New York, the Sacramento/San Joaquin River delta in California, the Gauley River in West Virginia, the Little River in North Carolina, the Cedar River in Iowa, the Upper Colorado River in Colorado, the Chetco River in Oregon, the Teton River in Idaho, the Monongahela River in Pennsylvania and the Coosa River in Alabama. These are not the most polluted rivers, only the ones under the greatest threat from future industry and development. There is no comparable list in Canada, though the Outdoor Recreation Council of British Columbia publishes an annual list of that province's most threatened creeks, streams and rivers.

more than 200 other species of birds, 31 species of mammals, and 44 species of reptiles and amphibians. No wonder the US Fish and Wildlife Service calls it "an oasis in an urban setting."

In addition to mollusks and crayfish, several fish species occupy freshwater "urban" marshes too. They lay their eggs in them. When those eggs hatch, the resulting fish swim into nearby urban rivers. Thus, residents of Philadelphia and Washington can now see perch, striped bass, catfish, sunfish and shad in their local waterways. But this is possible only because of what happened in Cleveland on the Cuyahoga. That fire was more than just a wake-up call to Ohioans; it alerted the residents of other states to the dangers of pollution too. So cities in those states took action as well.

In the James River, for example, which cuts through the southern city of Richmond, Virginia, bathers used to wear ear and nose plugs to stave off infections from sewage runoff. Today the river is stalked not just by people seeking a way to beat the summer heat, but also by blue herons chasing shad and catfish. In Chicago, residents can see sunfish and catfish in the Chicago River— goldfish too. When people tire of them as pets, they often throw them (thoughtlessly) into the Chicago, where—luckily for them—they thrive.

If Chicagoans look east into Lake Michigan, they'll see other kinds of aquatic life too: small-mouthed bass, yellow perch, lake trout, minnows and Pacific salmon. Yes, the same coho and chinook salmon that swim near Seattle were imported into the Great Lakes years ago as sport fish. They survive there, but their life cycles have been confused ever since.

There are Atlantic salmon in the Great Lakes as well. At one time they were so plentiful in Lake Ontario that you

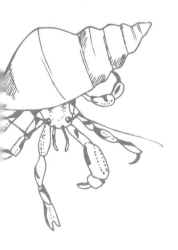

could stand on shore and fish for them with a pitchfork. Not anymore. With the building of cities like Toronto, Burlington and Hamilton on its northern, western and southern shores (what Ontarians call "the Golden Horseshoe"), salmon almost disappeared as a result of overfishing and **habitat degradation**. Now efforts are being made to restore them. Under a program developed by the Toronto Zoo, schoolchildren raise and hatch salmon eggs in classrooms and set the young salmon free in streams and rivers flowing into the lake. And it's working. If you stand at the edge of Lake Ontario along the Toronto shoreline, you might see a salmon or two among the walleye, perch and minnows that also swim in the shadow of the CN Tower.

This is undoubtedly good news for urban fish and their environment. But no matter how much things improve, urban aquatic life will never be as well off as their wild cousins. There are always significantly fewer fish in urban rivers, lakes and harbors than in wilderness waters, and they suffer more disease. The reason is simple: pollution, which, despite all those cleanups, remains a constant of urban life. But pollution means more than just chemicals. An equally harmful, though far less obvious, form of contamination is alien aquatic life: **invasive species** that were never meant to be anywhere near North America, but are here now—and multiplying in droves.

Sometimes these species were introduced deliberately. Consider those Chicago River goldfish and the Great Lakes Pacific salmon. But more often, introductions are accidental and invisible—until the harm they do is plain to everyone. When ships travel the world's oceans, they collect creatures in their ballast and transport them to places they don't belong, like New York, Montreal, Savannah and Oakland. As a result, North American harbors, coastlines, lakes and rivers are now teeming with species that compete with and, in some cases, destroy native wildlife. And that's a huge problem for everyone.

TOP: You can still catch fish from the boardwalk in Atlantic City, one of the most desirable properties in the original Monopoly board game. ATLANTIC CITY CONVENTION AND VISITORS AUTHORITY

BOTTOM: What you'll find beneath the boardwalk and in other coastal cities depends on how far out the tide has gone. CHRISTOPHER HARLEY

Examples are everywhere. The Asian clam, a teaspoon-sized animal with a shimmering yellow shell, is present in forty US states, where not only is it out-competing **native species** for food, but it's also clogging water systems to the point that in some states nuclear reactors have had to close temporarily. In Ohio and Tennessee, where clusters of the clams are present in gravel beds dredged for cement, the clams are mixed into the cement and render it useless.

The northern snakehead, an aggressive predatory fish from China, is now present in rivers throughout the United States, including the Potomac. Anyone catching one is advised to kill it straightaway because, crafty devil, it can live out of water too. It uses its fins to propel it on land, thus earning it the nickname "Frankenfish."

In Oregon, the European green crab devours native oysters, mussels, crabs, small fish, insects and just about anything else it can get its claws on. In San Francisco Bay, there are more than 230 alien marine species, making it one of the most invaded bodies of water in the world. In Florida, it's thought that 16 percent of all fish species are non-native. In fact, in every single estuary ever studied in the continental United States, there are at least 70 alien species.

One of these species, the zebra mussel, a fingernail-size mollusk from Asia, has wreaked havoc not just with the ecology of all five Great Lakes, but with their industry too. In some places, zebra mussel colonies have grown so dense that they've clogged urban and industrial pipelines to the point of preventing water flow from city water supplies and hydroelectric apparatuses. The problem is so bad that 95 percent of all the aquatic life in some stretches of the Illinois River is made up entirely of zebra mussels. The zebra's equally invasive cousin, the quagga mussel, has gone so far as to force turbines at Nevada's Hoover Dam to shut down temporarily, thus cutting power to more than 1.6 million customers.

The Asian carp, a rapacious silver fish that eats the same kind of food native trout and pike do, has become such a problem in the Mississippi River and Lake Calumet near Chicago that the state of Michigan recently sued the state of Illinois to force it to close canals linking the Mississippi to Lake Michigan as a way of keeping carp out of the lake. No wonder environmentalists call such infestations a "nightmare scenario."

But don't think such "invasions" work only one way. Every time a ship brings an invasive species from the Sea of Japan into Los Angeles harbor, it probably returns with a native North American species that can do as much harm to native Asian fauna as the Asian carp does here. As a consequence, and despite the best efforts of governments and environmentalists, urban waters the world over are ecological disaster zones where no one knows what will happen next. The natural world is under siege under the sea too, and when we live in cities, we see that firsthand.

What are people doing to curb the spread of invasive species?

Believe it or not, they're eating them. A US environmental organization called the Nature Conservancy has suggested that because humans are prepared to eat almost anything anywhere, they should eat marine species that do native environments harm. As a result, the US Fish and Wildlife Service is investigating the idea of harvesting Asian carp in the Mississippi River.

Meanwhile, the lionfish, a striped starburst of a venomous fish that has devastated reefs along the Florida coast, is now being served in braised fillets at the South Gate restaurant in New York City. And if you think the idea is far-fetched, consider that it wasn't that long ago that no one dreamed of eating dandelion leaves. Now they're haute cuisine.

Chapter Four

Our Feathered Friends—The Birds

You may recall that the first chapter of this book held up the raccoon as a possible poster animal for today's urban critter. Raccoons are such adaptable creatures that they've taken to urban living like a New York billionaire. The city is their oyster, and everywhere you look they're prying it open in search of another pearl. But could there be a better candidate for the ultimate urban animal? The super city specialist? Believe it or not, yes. Or at least maybe. Look outside and you might see a black bird shuffling along a telephone wire. Or a smaller brown and gray one pecking at the ground. Or a grayish white one yelling his head off. While they may not exude the same city cool as a raccoon, there are five bird species who fit just as neatly into the urban landscape as that wily four-footed bandit. This chapter is about them.

Sadly, urban skies no longer boast as many birds as they once did. Their numbers have dropped steeply in recent years because of habitat loss, pesticide use and climate change. Birds also die in large numbers when they fly into buildings (see page 67)

OPPOSITE: City skies are home to many different bird species, including several raptors, or birds of prey. This peregrine falcon built a nest atop a hospital in suburban Toronto.
WILLIAM OSLER HEALTH SYSTEM, ETOBICOKE GENERAL HOSPITAL, ETOBICOKE, ONTARIO

or the claws and teeth of pet cats. No one knows how many birds are killed each year by domestic cats, but it's significant. Consequently, it's no longer unusual to look up at an urban sky and not see a single bird.

However, there are also moments when a flock of crows (called a murder) suddenly takes off and the sky is filled with wings. Or when too many starlings to count line up on a telephone wire like gargoyles. Or when the chirping, squawking and peeping of worried bird parents watching their young fly for the first time in late spring or early summer is almost loud enough to drown out car noise. Almost.

But as with mammals, only certain kinds of birds really take to city life. There are 914 species native to North America, and many live in urban areas. Yet only two, the crow and the gull, have managed to insert themselves wholeheartedly into urban life. Three others, the starling, the house sparrow and the rock pigeon, arrived from elsewhere—Europe and the Middle East—but they, too, have taken to North American cities like…well…ducks to water. (More about waterfowl in Chapter Five.) Even if you know nothing about birds, you probably can recognize one or two of these five bird species—maybe even all five—simply because they're so common. If you live in a city or town and you notice a bird flying by, chances are it's a starling, a house sparrow, a rock pigeon, a crow or a gull.

That's not to say other native species don't live in cities as well. You might be familiar with American robins (what some poets have called "robin red breast"), cardinals (the scarlet namesakes of St. Louis's major-league baseball team), and barn swallows (their long forked tails make them look as if they're wearing tuxedos). As well,

What are some other common urban bird species?

There are too many to list here, and the birds you see in your backyard will depend on where in North America you live. It also will depend on the time of year, since many birds fly south for the winter. Nevertheless, some bird species common in the spring and summer include the blue jay, bluebird, Baltimore oriole (the state bird of Maryland), American goldfinch, black-capped chickadee, common grackle, meadowlark, house finch, ruby-throated hummingbird, northern mockingbird, red-breasted nuthatch, purple martin, tree swallow, red-bellied woodpecker, Brewer's blackbird and the northern flicker. Merlin and sharp-shinned hawks are also becoming common customers at bird feeders in winter. Because of these feeders, the size of their winter range has increased.

Canada geese and many kinds of duck species live in or near urban ponds, as do great blue herons. These magnificent blue-gray fisher birds with their long ballerina legs and tent-stake beaks are always worth a head turn, not just because they're so awe-inspiring, but because they're so surprisingly widespread. As long as a city has some sort of pond in it—some marshy ground where a heron can get its feet wet and poke around for fish—that city probably will have herons too. What's certain, however, is that cities will always have many more starlings, house sparrows, rock pigeons, crows and gulls.

As already mentioned, three of these five bird types aren't native to North America. The starling and house sparrow arrived from Europe—mainly Britain—and the rock pigeon (most people simply call them pigeons) from the deserts of North Africa and the Middle East. Immigrants brought them, by accident and design.

Immigrating to a new country can be a bewildering experience. Two hundred years ago it was even more unsettling because there was a good chance you'd never see the country where you were born again. So when immigrants arrived in North America—what they called the New World—in the 1800s, they often found it strange and frightening. To make it more familiar, British and other settlers brought mementos of the Old World—the world they left behind. They brought furniture, paintings, various other decorative objects and birds. Not pets, but birds they could set free into the North American sky. That way, they figured, they could hear the same birdsong in their new homes as they did in their old ones.

But which birds to bring? They found their answer in the plays of William Shakespeare. Because the starling is mentioned—once—in a play called *Henry IV*, an organization

TOP: Pigeons have adapted so well to city living that they can even be found in Times Square in Manhattan.
COLIN MILLS

BOTTOM: Barred owls are one of a number of species of urban raptors who prey on urban rodents.
CHRISTIAN LAUB

OPPOSITE: Cities are often home to great blue herons, as long as there are places for them to get their long legs wet and poke around for fish.
ROBIN BASSETT

Some interesting facts about pigeons

1) Pigeons don't rely on their eyes to find their way home. Instead they tap into the Earth's magnetic fields. They also use cues based on the position of the sun.

2) Egyptian hieroglyphics suggest pigeons were domesticated more than five thousand years ago, which means as long as there has been human civilization, there probably have been pigeons.

3) Rock pigeons carried information for the US Army Signal Corps during the First and Second World Wars, so it's possible that they may have had a hand (or toe) in saving human lives.

4) After returning from his five-year voyage on the *Beagle*, Charles Darwin, the father of the theory of evolution, kept pigeons because he found that the huge differences between captive breeds and wild pigeons helped him formulate some aspects of his theory.

called the Acclimatization Society, which helped immigrants adjust to the new continent, decided to release a hundred European starlings into New York's Central Park in 1890. The house sparrow (also known as the English sparrow) got its North American entrée the same way. Shakespeare compared sparrows to angels that could awaken dreamers from feathery beds; so they had to come too—to Brooklyn in 1851. And since the Swan of Avon, as Shakespeare is known, was always writing about pigeons—in *Hamlet*, *The Merchant of Venice*, *Love's Labours Lost*, *As You Like It* and *Titus Andronicus*—they also were considered essential to civilized living. Luckily for British immigrants, they were already here. Most likely they arrived on a merchant ship two hundred years earlier.

But it's precisely because starlings, sparrows and pigeons were brought to live in North America's then-new cities that they were able to thrive in them. When European settlers created urban spaces—towns and cities—for themselves, they created habitats unsuitable to many native birds. But such spaces were familiar to the three new interlopers because they came from places like London, Birmingham and Manchester. Consequently, when they arrived in New York, Philadelphia or Boston, they were able to move in with little difficulty—or competition.

The starling, an omnipresent black bird whose wings are frosted with tiny white flakes in the fall, is that rare wild bird who doesn't mind large groups of people. And what are cities if not large groups of people? And even though insects are a starling's favorite food, they—like raccoons, skunks and rats—eat many other kinds of food too. And as you now know, that willingness to adapt and make do with whatever's put in front of them is a hallmark of the successful city critter.

But the starling's adaptability goes well beyond diet. When it's cold, they warm themselves under neon lights. What could be more urban than that? And they're not at all particular about where they nest. They'll use almost any kind of cavity to raise chicks, including dryer, oven and bathroom vents, lampposts and bridge abutments. That's important because starlings nest a lot. They can have two or three broods a year, and they're dutiful parents. They pay a lot more attention to their young than many other bird species do, so their chicks tend to survive more than those of many other species. Is it any wonder they're so numerous?

But most important, starlings are smart, and like their relatives, the famous talking Mynah birds, they're excellent mimics, so they can communicate with and, if necessary, confuse other birds. In fact, starlings are thought to be capable of imitating the calls of twenty-three other kinds of birds. Think what an advantage that can be. Suppose, for example, you were a starling and you wanted to nest in a particular hollow of a particular tree, but a pair of chickadees got there first. There may not be a hawk nearby, but if you could imitate one, those chickadees might vanish like yesterday's lunch. Then—*voilà!*—the hollow would be yours. You might say their gift for mimicry gives starlings something to crow about.

House sparrows, small brown and gray birds about the size of your fist, thrive in cities for similar reasons. Though seeds are a sparrow's primary food source—and think how many different kinds of seeds there are in urban gardens, on vacant lots, in bird feeders and in parks—they, like starlings, will eat pretty much anything else too. In fact, sparrows are so unfussy that according to the *Texas State Handbook* (house sparrows were declared a protected species in Texas in 1883) they'll eat 830 different kinds of food. (You have to wonder who counted them.)

TOP: Barn swallows earned their name from their fondness for nesting in barns. Today they'll also nest in carports and boathouses, but mercifully no one has suggested renaming them carport swallows. WAYNE CAMPBELL

BOTTOM: The first starling arrived in New York in 1890. Now they're everywhere. WAYNE CAMPBELL

OPPOSITE: Urban birds can turn up anywhere—even on outboard motors. CATHERINE BELL

TOP: Two of the most common birds in North America's urban skies are the gull (often called the seagull) and the crow. They're found almost everywhere, even side by side. JOHN FERGUSON

MIDDLE: Crows are native to North America and are considered songbirds, despite the caw/screech sound they make. JUTTA SCHULZ

Not surprisingly, sparrows are usually first in line when someone brings a bag of popcorn—or practically anything else—to scatter in a park. And because sparrows have lived among humans for centuries—long before they arrived in North America—they, too, are used to nesting in human-made structures like the eaves of houses. Almost any old nook or cranny will do.

Rock pigeons, those striped bluish gray birds about the size of a man's foot, are so comfortable in urban areas that there probably isn't a city or town in the world where they aren't found. Some, like the pigeons in London's Trafalgar Square or Venice's Piazza San Marco, are famous. Feeding the pigeons outside St. Mark's Cathedral is as much a part of a visit to Venice as riding a gondola. And what do Venetian pigeons eat? The same thing pigeons everywhere else eat: seeds and fruits. But like starlings, sparrows and other urban generalists, they're not particular. If humans want to toss them some pizza crust, popcorn, peanuts, sandwich pieces or cake, they'll eat that too. Also like starlings and sparrows (and raccoons and skunks), pigeons are perfectly comfortable building nests in cities—on structures built by people. Whether it's a newly built million-dollar show home or a derelict warehouse, pigeons don't mind. Even the underside of a bridge will suffice. Windowsills, grain elevators (in small towns) and barns are all places you might find pigeon nests.

Crows and gulls are similarly adaptable birds, which is why they are about as familiar on most urban streetscapes as a McDonald's or a bus stop. But unlike the starling, sparrow and pigeon, crows and gulls have been in North America for as long as people can remember—probably longer—because both are native to this continent. It's just that now, with the proliferation of cities and suburbs, their profile is greater than it's ever been before.

Crows, like their wilderness cousins the ravens—and those British immigrants the starlings—are extremely smart (see below to find out how smart). They're also adaptable and omnivorous, meaning they'll eat just about anything, which is what they'll find in a city. Like raccoons, crows are adept at forcing things open to find food inside. They're also fearless. Humans, dogs, cats, even cars—none of them scares a crow. Consequently, these coal-black, foot-long songbirds (yes, despite the ear-splitting "caw caw" sound they make, crows are considered songbirds by people who classify birds) have no problem surviving in cities. Some people might even say they rule the urban avian roost.

A lot of people call gulls—a white or pale gray web-footed bird—seagulls, but that's incorrect because it suggests they live only by the sea. We may associate a gull's call with the sound of waves and the tangy scent of salt air, but gulls can live almost anywhere, providing there's a large body of water nearby. That means they live throughout North America. And like other urban birds, gulls eat almost anything: garbage, carrion (a polite word for dead animals), live worms, mice, eggs, other birds (as long as they're smaller) and fish. Have you ever ridden a ferry and watched gulls circle overhead? They're watching for food. They've learned that ferries are a great source of sustenance thanks to the generous passengers on board.

ABOVE: On top of everything else, crows are smart. Smart enough to hold a grudge. If you cross one, you'll never hear the end of it. WAYNE CAMPBELL

OPPOSITE BOTTOM: Gulls don't have to live by the sea, though thousands do. All they need to survive is some kind of body of water. WAYNE CAMPBELL

Amazing Animal Adaptation

Some scientists say crows are as smart as parrots and great apes. They certainly are excellent problem solvers. Like the apes and us, they'll use tools to extract food from tight spots. They've also figured out what red and green traffic lights mean: a red light means they can feel safe swooping down onto a road and eating whatever's there, and a green light means they should fly back to their perch and wait. Like parrots, crows can imitate the sounds of other animals and learn to associate those sounds with actions, like gathering food and announcing danger. They're also smart enough that they'll hold a grudge. If you've ever made the grievous mistake of disturbing a crow or, worse, a crow's chick, that crow won't let you forget it soon. The next time you dare show your head, one of the crow pair (they mate for life) will probably dive-bomb you like a kamikaze pilot. And the bombing can go on for weeks.

Toss a French fry into the air and you can bet a gull will be hovering some-where overhead to grab it.

Of course, it's not as if you won't find other bird species living in North American cities too. You will. But because they don't adapt as well to city life as the übersuccessful starling, sparrow, pigeon, crow and gull, they're not as common. You have to look harder for them, and you have to know where to look.

The American robin, for example, that famous first face of spring, is native to large parts of North America, especially where there is, or was, a forest. But it, too, has been touched by European influence. There is a smaller, though similar, red-breasted bird called the robin who is native to the United Kingdom and northern Europe. So when homesick British immigrants saw the American robin's brick-red breast feathers (actually only the male's feathers turn red; the female's remain brownish), they embraced it as America's robin, even though biologically the two birds aren't related.

Cardinals—bright red birds with jet-black facemasks (like raccoons, they resemble bandits)—also got their common name from Europe. In the Catholic Church, cardinals, who are second in power only to the pope, wear red robes similar in color to the feathers of these North American red birds. So when immigrants caught their first sight of what's now called the cardinal, they thought of home—and Rome. The cardinal (also called the redbird) is now such a beloved figure in America that it's become the state bird of seven US states and, as mentioned earlier, the nickname of St. Louis's major-league baseball team. They're also more widespread in North America than nature intended them to be thanks to the spread of cities and all the birdseed city residents leave in feeders.

Swallows are also native to North America, but with the arrival of European settlers, they assumed an extra name. They're now called barn swallows because of their fondness for nesting in barns. In the wilderness, swallows nest in caves, but when settlers built barns in rural America and southern Canada, swallows nested in them. So the two were linked, like cake and icing or baseball and peanuts. Today, North Americans build many other kinds of hollowed-out structures like boathouses and carports, and barn swallows nest in them as well. Mercifully, however, no one has suggested changing the barn swallow's name to the carport swallow.

It's only natural to think of songbirds like these when we think of urban birds because there are so many more of them in cities than there are birds of prey. You hardly ever see flocks of owls, eagles, falcons or hawks darken a city sky, though interestingly, in some eastern cities and only during the fall, you can see dozens, even hundreds, of broad-winged hawks take flight when they begin their annual **migration** to South America. (It's quite a sight.) But if you think of how nature's food chains work, it's only logical that there be many more prey animals—like songbirds—in the world. After all, a single predatory bird will eat dozens of songbirds a year, so the bigger and hungrier the predator, the fewer there will be. There simply isn't enough food for more. Consequently, just as cities contain many skunks and raccoons, far fewer coyotes and only the odd mountain lion, they are home to many more songbirds than birds of prey.

Even so, it's not as if raptors—the generic name for predatory birds—don't live in cities too. It's just that, as with those very rare mountain lions, they can be tricky to see. For example, there probably isn't a decent-sized city in all North America that isn't home to at least one pair of great horned owls, a fierce tawny-colored hunter with hornlike tufts of feathers on its head and a wingspan of up to 4.5 feet (1.33 meters). Imagine one of those swooping into your backyard. It's not as unlikely as you think, given that big North American cities, with their many wooded parks, golf courses and cemeteries, are full of animals that great horned owls eat. Animals such as rabbits, rats, mice, squirrels, skunks (owls, unlike humans, don't appear to mind their odor), ducks, geese, herons, crows, jays, small hawks and smaller owls. They'll even eat domestic cats. So it stands to reason that great horned owls will set up house in cities too. But because there aren't many,

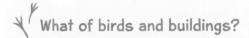

What of birds and buildings?

The very structures cities are made of—the buildings, bridges, even cell-phone towers—can be deadly to birds because they fly into them, especially the lighted windows in skyscrapers, and die. In fact, scientists say colliding with large buildings is the second-largest threat to North American birds after habitat loss. Every year more than a billion birds are said to lose their lives by striking skyscrapers. That's why an organization in Chicago now deploys more than eighty volunteers each morning during the spring and/or fall migrations to search the city's streets for victims of window strikes.

ABOVE: Because owls are nocturnal, it's hard to see them in city skies. But that doesn't mean they're not there.
WAYNE CAMPBELL

TOP: Peregrine falcons can be found in many North American cities because they eat rock pigeons, and cities teem with those. BOB HOLLAND

BOTTOM: Bald eagles are opportunistic birds who will take food wherever they can find it, even the city dump. WAYNE CAMPBELL

OPPOSITE TOP: Cardinals got their name from their bright red feathers, which reminded European immigrants of the robes worn by cardinals in the Catholic Church. COLIN MILLS

and because they usually hunt at dawn or dusk, seeing one isn't nearly as easy as seeing a pigeon.

Cities are home to barred owls too. These are smaller grayish owls named for the dark brown bars of feathers along their upper breasts. Before cities were built, barred owls lived in Canada's vast boreal forests and the deciduous forests of the eastern United States. But when parts of these forests were destroyed to make way for cities and suburbs, instead of being displaced, the barred owl adapted. Like other urban critters, they realized that suburban living suited them. There were still trees and tree stumps with hollows in them for nests, and all kinds of food too: mice, voles, moles, rabbits, chipmunks, shrews, squirrels, small foxes and possums—not to mention a raft of songbirds. In fact, as suburbs spread across America, so did the barred owl. Now the barred owl's range extends right across to the Pacific, and they have people—and cities—to thank for it.

Some urban areas are even home to nesting pairs of bald eagles, the national symbol of the United States. It just so happens that a good many of these areas are in Canada because it's only in British Columbia and Alaska that the proud white-hooded bird is still found in significant numbers. Even so, some continue to live in the US northwest in cities like Seattle and Olympia, and farther east too. (The Introduction mentioned several pairs nesting in Philadelphia.) In early 2010 a bald eagle made news in Portland, Oregon, when he crashed into a two-story house in the city's Columbia Park district. Upon hearing the noise, the homeowner was too afraid to go outside because she thought she was being burgled. You can't blame her. The idea that a bird as big as a bald eagle would live in a city like Portland can be difficult to imagine, but like all successful urban animals, bald eagles are—here's that word again—adaptable. So it makes sense that they'd live in urban areas too.

Like all successful urban critters, bald eagles eat many different kinds of foods, including foods we humans throw out. We may not like to picture the national emblem of America—the majestic winged figure on the US silver dollar, the half dollar and the quarter—scrounging grub from a garbage dump, but they do. Why wouldn't they if it's available to them? Scavenging requires a lot less energy than hunting does. (Remember those fat, lazy landfill bears from Chapter One?) However, it may be reassuring to know that bald eagles also fish for salmon and herring, and, given the chance, will grab a duck in mid-air. As befits their image, they're powerful hunters. Trouble is, they sometimes assert that image in urban parks by going after heron chicks—a move decidedly unpopular with humans. Also, as is typical of many urban critters, bald eagles don't mind nesting in urban areas. Be it a large urban tree or a tower in a power line, they're not bothered as long as people don't bother them.

Peregrine falcons have become attuned to urban living too. They'll build nests on apartment buildings, hospital roofs, bridges, church steeples, anywhere a suitable ledge can be found that resembles a cliff top. That wasn't so forty years ago. Back then you'd almost never see a peregrine falcon in the city, and hardly any in the country because of the devastating effects DDT and other pesticides had on them. These deadly poison cocktails worked their way into falcon eggshells and made them too fragile to survive incubation. Therefore, hardly any falcon chicks were born. Now that DDT and other pesticides have been banned in large parts of the continent, the peregrine falcon—one of the fastest birds on Earth (it can reach speeds of 200 miles per hour or 320 kilometers per hour in an aerial dive)—has been saved.

Today, a good number have found city living to their taste, which is why you'll see them in New York, Chicago, Toronto,

What are the biggest and smallest flying birds in North America?

The bird with the largest wingspan in North America is the highly endangered California condor. When its black wings are outstretched, they can reach a full 10 feet (3 meters) from tip to tip. The smallest bird is the calliope hummingbird, which is only about 2 inches (5 centimeters) long and weighs 8/100 of an ounce (2.5 grams). It's found only in western parts of the continent.

BOTTOM: Sparrows will eat almost any kind of food humans throw away. No wonder urban skies are so full of them. LAURA COX

San Francisco, Los Angeles, Montreal—almost any large city you can name. And when you learn what they eat, you'll know why: rock pigeons. Because if there's one bird species all North American cities have in abundance, it's the rock pigeon. So with all that easy prey around, is it any wonder that peregrine falcons live in cities too?

A couple of hawk species have followed a similar path. The red-tailed hawk and the Cooper's hawk, both medium-sized birds and both good hunters, have, like falcons, learned to move with city rhythms. The Cooper's hawk, a bird with blue-gray feathers and a long tail, eats pigeons, mourning doves, different kinds of songbirds (jays, robins, starlings and sparrows) and even rodents, all of whom are found within city limits. It's because Cooper's hawks like to nest so high up in urban trees that people don't always know they're there.

The red-tailed hawk, named for its solid red tail (the rest of it is brown), uses telephone and power poles, playing-field lights and metal power towers to perch on and get a bird's-eye view of what's going on in the urban area below. And that includes what might be available for dinner.

Eagles, falcons and hawks living side by side with skyscrapers and bridge traffic is now a fairly common phenomenon in North America, but it's also a fairly new one. Just as coyotes weren't always present in many cities, neither were birds of prey. As recently as 1991, New York City residents were so astounded by the presence of a male red-tailed hawk in Manhattan's concrete forest that he became the subject of a PBS television documentary narrated by Oscar-winning actress Joanne Woodward. Named Pale Male because of his cream-colored breast feathers, he went on to establish his own urban hawk dynasty from the ledge of a high-priced, high-rise condo overlooking Central Park. But when he first appeared, Pale Male was such an extraordinary sight that each morning, long before sunrise, throngs of spectators would gather in the

ABOVE: Red-tailed hawks often use telephone and power poles to get a bird's-eye view of the urban landscape below. WAYNE CAMPBELL

Amazing Animal Adaptation

Pale Male isn't New York's only renowned red-tailed hawk. In the spring of 2011, the *New York Times*, that city's highly esteemed newspaper of record, mounted a web cam on a twelfth-floor ledge outside the office of the president of New York University. A pair of red-tailed hawks had built a nest there, and thanks to the web cam, the whole online world could watch them fuss over three speckled buff-white eggs. The university's president, John Sexton, was quoted saying, "To be two feet away and look at their talons and their eyes and their beaks and their beautiful feathers, it puts you in touch with the transcendent."

Trouble was, this wild pair fit a little too neatly into urban living to suit the tastes of some viewers. Violet and Bobby, as they were christened, kept lining their nest with distinctly unnatural materials, such as a thick sheet of white plastic, a soiled hand towel, and artificial Easter grass, meaning their finished nest was anything but pristine. So people complained. Loudly enough for an NYU assistant professor of sociology and environmental studies to come to Violet and Bobby's defense. According to Colin Jerolmack, birds like red-tailed hawks have no innate appreciation for what's "natural" and what's not; to them, there is no such distinction. And that, he added, "is perhaps one of the greatest lessons they can teach us."

park with binoculars and telescopes to watch him start his day. At the time, they didn't want to miss what they believed would be their one and only chance to see him. They didn't realize then that he was showing them the future.

That's as good an illustration as any of how the world of urban wildlife continues to evolve. Animals who scientists never thought could make it in the urban jungle suddenly appear on its fringes, then move to its middle. (Recall that gray whale who turned up in the center of Vancouver.) This is true of bird species too. The latest surprise in the urban sky is the osprey, or as it's also known, the sea hawk or fish eagle. Until recently, these large dark brown and white raptors (the biggest ones have wingspans of up to 6.5 feet or 2 meters) were thought to embody the wild and unsullied world of clear and pristine waterways. No more. Even they have decided to give urban living a try, and so far their efforts have been rewarded. As long as there's a ready supply of fish in an urban area and some clear water—even a large creek—the osprey will find a way of making do (which is why you won't find many in Kansas).

Helping them along is the fact that they'll nest on almost anything. As long as ospreys have some sort of firm perch on which to build their nests, they're happy, and that's why you see osprey nests on everything from power poles to bridges to docks to buoys. Any kind of medium-sized fish will do for dinner too. For an example of just how opportunistic ospreys are, one only has to return to Portland, Oregon, where, in the old part of the city in what's left of its original Chinatown, there is a classical Chinese garden called the Lan Su Chinese Garden. In English, it's called the Garden of Awakening Orchids. However, it could just as easily be called the Garden of the Greedy Osprey because of the big brown and white bird who feeds regularly on the ornamental goldfish in its concrete pond. This osprey takes so many goldfish each year that the pond has to be restocked every spring. And none of the new fish ever gets to reach its full size because the osprey eats them first. (The Seattle Aquarium loses trout to a heron the same way.)

Years ago, the sight of a bird like an osprey might have frightened some city folk. Today, people still stare at them, but with wonder not fear. To think that an osprey, a bald eagle or a red-tailed hawk like Pale Male could feel comfortable in a city like Portland or New York seems miraculous. But if we take the time to understand how birds survive in cities, we'll realize that what we're seeing is nature itself adapting to a new and strange (but less so all the time) environment.

What are parrots doing in southern California?

Only one parrot species has ever been native to North America. It was called the Carolina parakeet, and by 1939 it had been hunted to extinction. Yet today there are thirteen parrot species living in urban centers in southern California because people adopt parrots as pets, find they're too much trouble to look after and let them go. Parrots have been flying around Greater Los Angeles since the 1960s and are now an established part of the LA aviary. Some are as colorful—and noticeable—as rainbows. Because of that, they illustrate perhaps better than any other kind of animal species the infinite capacity of people to move wildlife around the planet for economic, social or purely decorative reasons.

ABOVE: Until recently, ospreys embodied the unsullied world of wild waterways. Not anymore. Even they have decided to give urban living a try.
MARK GAUDIO

73

Chapter Five

Like Water Off a Duck's Back— Birds Who Swim

You probably won't remember it, but there's a good chance the first time anyone pointed out a wild animal to you was at your local park. There's also a strong possibility that the animal being pointed out was a duck. Urban ponds are full of ducks, and feeding them is something many people— including parents of young children—like to do. You've probably seen them yourself: moms and dads showing ducks to children barely old enough to walk, and making quacking noises as they do. Well, maybe there was a time years ago when you were that child and it was your mom or dad quacking at you. We don't realize it at the time, but that moment, when we take our first wide-eyed look at ducks flapping their way across a park pond, is often our introduction to urban wildlife. It's the moment when our parents first say to us: "Hey, look, there's a wild animal who lives in our city." They probably don't use those words, but that's what they mean.

For that reason, ducks—and geese and swans—deserve a chapter of their own in a book about city critters. There may

OPPOSITE: Birds who live on or near fresh water are part of the urban landscape too. Canada geese are almost as common in many cities as squirrels. WAYNE CAMPBELL

not be as many ducks, geese and swans in cities as there are pigeons and crows, and they may not be as glamorous as bald eagles (well, maybe swans are), but like pigeons and crows, they're birds everyone knows. And the ducks, geese and swans we in North America know best are the mallard duck, the Canada goose and the mute swan. You'd be hard-pressed to find a city anywhere in the United States and Canada that isn't home to at least one, and often all three.

The mallard is so common that when most people think of a duck, the duck they think of (whether they know it or not) is the mallard. You can probably picture one with a little help. If there's a pair of them, the female is the dowdier one. That's because in the world of birds, males show off to females, and one way they do that is to array themselves in bright, eye-catching plumage.

Why do you think peacocks are so proud? Consequently, the female mallard's feathers are a plain-looking blend of mousy brown and off-white. Even her bill is brown. Her only visible splash of color is on her feet. They're pumpkin orange.

In contrast, the male mallard is far showier. His bill is lemon yellow; his head is an iridescent blend of cobalt blue and teal; at his neckline is a pale but distinguished off-white necklace; and his breast is a rich shade of chestnut brown, or maroon. His wings and tail feathers are plain brown and white, like the female's, with some black. But his webbed feet are bright orange too. Next time you're at your local park, see if you can identify a mallard pair. If it's spring, they'll probably have ducklings too.

Why are mallards so common? The main reason is that, like all successful urban critters, they're generalists. As long as there's enough water nearby, they're happy eating a wide variety of foods, and as you know by now, that's a trademark of city living. Also, when early settlers to North America cleared forests for timber and farmland, they gave mallards an inadvertent boost. Suddenly what had been purely a prairie duck had vast new territories to conquer.

Those same settlers also decided that mallards were ideal for hunting, so they moved them around from place to place so they could shoot them. Later, when cities were incorporated and duck hunting was outlawed inside those cities, mallards who had managed to keep their heads were given a free pass. For the first time, they were able to breed and multiply without the risk of being shot at. No wonder their numbers took off. Now it's left to other urban predators like raccoons, skunks, coyotes and raptors to keep mallard populations under control by eating their eggs and their offspring. Mallards lay up to a dozen eggs at a time, because nature knows most hatchlings won't survive long enough to have ducklings of their own.

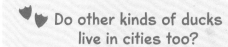

Do other kinds of ducks live in cities too?

Yes. Many. Twenty-eight different duck species are native to North America. What kind of duck they are depends on where on the continent they live, but many North American cities are home to wood ducks, ring-necked ducks, northern pintails, canvasbacks, lesser and greater scaups and American black ducks.

ABOVE: Often ducks don't have to travel far for their food because visitors to city parks are so willing to feed them. DARCY MANN

Mallards have wings, so if they wanted to, they could fly away from any urban area at any time. But most don't because cities are full of food. Think of all those people—those parents of young children, and others—who buy birdseed to scatter in city parks. All urban ducks have to do is flap their wings, waddle around a bit, shake their tails and look cute, and a member of another species (a human) will throw them dinner. You can bet that never happens in the wild. So why blow a setup like that?

But what if the handouts dry up? Urban mallards have that figured too. They choose loafing areas near rivers, seacoasts or farmers' fields, so if they need a meal, they can always fly to one of those sites to get one. Then when their stomachs are full, they can return to their urban park or garden where, because hunting is prohibited, they'll be safe overnight.

Flying back and forth this way is easy for mallards because before they were city stalwarts, they were major migrators.

Amazing Animal Adaptation

Don't mention "bird brains" to former Vancouver community police officer Ray Petersen—not after his encounter with a mother mallard duck. Petersen, who is now retired from the force, was walking under one of the city's bridges when the duck appeared from nowhere and grabbed his pant leg. Then she let go and started waddling around quacking. Petersen thought she was "a bit goofy" so he shoved her away. But the duck was determined; she wouldn't take no for an answer. So making sure she still had Petersen's eye, she waddled up the road and lay down on a storm sewer grate. Petersen thought nothing of that either, until the duck grabbed him again when he started walking away.

Realizing something was afoot, he followed her to the sewer grate and looked down. Below the heavy steel grate, swimming round and round in the water that had collected there, were eight tiny helpless ducklings. So Petersen phoned his police sergeant, who arrived at the scene and phoned two other constables. When they arrived, the mother duck quacked and ran around them too. Then she lay down on a nearby curb and watched as the two constables arranged for a tow truck to lift the grate from the sewer. Using a vegetable strainer, they rescued the ducklings one by one and delivered them to their mother. When all eight were safe, she quacked farewell to the officers and marched them to a nearby inlet, where they jumped into the water and swam away. The incident changed Petersen's mind about ducks, he said afterward. He thinks they're a lot smarter than he used to. And while he never ate duck before, he wouldn't dream of it now.

They flew south each winter and north each spring. Now, thanks to that ready supply of urban food and the fact that climate change is making winters less severe in more and more northern cities, they prefer to stay put. In some cities, such as those in the Pacific Northwest, California and throughout the US Sunbelt, it never—or hardly ever—snows, so why would an urban duck expend a lot of energy flying somewhere else?

You can bet they don't stick around too long in places like Winnipeg, where the temperature can still drop to minus 40 degrees Fahrenheit/Celsius. Yet even in cities like Toronto, where it does snow and winters can still be fairly tough, you'll find mallards in January. Why? It's that steady food supply. Mallards and other urban ducks figure if they're patient enough, they can wait out bad times. In fact, if you visit a Toronto pond in the middle of January, you might see a flock of mallards—and other duck species—huddled like football players. By keeping close, they not only look cute, but also lessen the windchill. They also keep their feet busy, paddling, paddling and paddling, without going anywhere. But by doing so, they keep the pond from freezing. And you can bet when people see them huddled together that way, looking so cold and pitiful ("Aw, look at those poor duckies!"), they're going to throw them more food. Mission accomplished.

Canada geese are another kind of urban waterfowl who, in many cases, have decided that flying south each winter is for the birds. Or not. It depends on the goose. Think about where you live. Maybe each year you can see Vs of them flying south in the fall and north in the spring. But at the same time, there also may be other Canada geese who never go anywhere, except from one urban park to another.

Why is this? Not surprisingly, people are the cause. Decades ago, hunters identified these large upright birds with pale brown body feathers, a long black neck and a white wimple around

TOP: Ducks are among the first kinds of urban wildlife that people notice... probably because they're so easy to spot. HEATHER FLATT

BOTTOM: Canada geese are so numerous in urban parks that city officials sometimes relocate goslings to faraway places in hopes of making them stay away. But it rarely works. BLAIR COX

TOP: The droppings Canada geese leave have made them unpopular with many city dwellers to the point that some city residents want them culled. WAYNE CAMPBELL

BOTTOM: When their eggs hatch, Canada geese mothers have to show their offspring how to find food... something that's often easy in cities. WAYNE CAMPBELL

their chins as highly desirable game birds. But they could only shoot them at certain times of the year—in the fall when they headed south, and in the spring on their way north. But that wasn't enough for avid hunters, so they decided to do nature one better. They began moving different subspecies of Canada geese—there are eleven in North America—to places they didn't belong. They thought that because different subspecies of geese migrate at different times of the year, having different types in one place would lengthen the hunting season.

That may have seemed a good idea at the time, but, as always, there were consequences. Nature evolves for a reason, and when humans interfere with evolution, things can go wrong. In this case, members of one goose subspecies began breeding with members of another, and a whole new kind of Canada goose was born. Except this Canada goose was perfectly happy not to migrate anywhere because there was no need to.

Depending on where the goose lived, it may have been warm year-round, so there was no reason to escape to a kinder environment. And even in the worst of weather, North American cities have a way of keeping Canada geese fed—with grass. You'll recall from the chapter about skunks that one thing every North American city has more than enough of is grass. Even in deserts, where water is as precious as life itself, people waste vast amounts watering lawns, cemeteries and golf courses. In winter, thanks to various artificial fertilizers, if city lawns aren't covered with snow, they remain a decent shade of green. And to a Canada goose, that's heaven. Imagine if everywhere you looked there were great chocolate lawns spreading in different directions. Now you know how an urban Canada goose feels. The only other thing they need is fresh water, and since many city parks and golf courses have ponds, that's as good as it gets for a goose. Is it any wonder so many call cities home?

Too many, some people would say, because unlike mallards, who drop their waste discreetly by the sides of ponds where humans won't notice it, Canada geese treat city lawns like toilets. They can't help it; that's how their plumbing works. Consequently, wherever there are "gaggles" of geese, there are globs of goose droppings—minefields of them—that force us to watch our step…or else! This preponderance of gross green goo has led some people to suggest culling urban geese. But in the United States and Canada there are laws protecting migratory birds, so it's not as straightforward a proposal as you might think. Not only that—because our attitudes to hunting have changed, many people find the notion of killing an animal for something as trivial as fouling a lawn barbaric.

So what's a city wildlife official to do? Recently, some have begun picking up goose eggs and shaking them so the embryos inside can't develop. This means the eggs never hatch and the mothers end up sitting on them long after the normal twenty-eight-day incubation period is over. Poor mothers, but at least no more urban geese are born. If that doesn't work, young goslings (what goose chicks are called) may be relocated to places far away. Officials hope by doing this the geese will resume a natural migratory life. But things don't always work out that way. Many geese find their way home, and home is where they stay. All this makes life very tricky for beleaguered officials charged with solving a city's Canada goose problem.

The swan, that graceful white lyre of a bird who drifts elegantly over city ponds like a decoration, is another familiar urban dweller. At least the mute swan is. North America has two migratory species as well: the trumpeter and the tundra swan. At up to 35 pounds (16 kilograms), the trumpeter swan is the largest waterfowl species in the world. Tundra swans are smaller, but the sight of either species pumping their milk-white wings against a bright blue sky, is one to savor. It's nature at her most splendid. However, because trumpeter and tundra swans are not normally urban birds, they're rare sights in cities. Hence they're not the swans you see when you visit your local park.

TOP: One of the reasons cities are so popular with certain kinds of waterfowl is that people are often ready sources of food. WAYNE CAMPBELL

BOTTOM:. Many mute swans have their wings clipped so they won't be able to fly away from urban parks, where they act as decoration. But others manage to escape that fate. LAURA COX

Are there any common urban sea birds?

Yes. Regardless of whether you live on the east, west or Gulf coast of North America, you have a good chance of seeing a double-crested cormorant, especially in winter. Even if you live inland, you might see them in summer because most migrate inland to breed. They fly to lakes and slow-moving rivers across the north-central United States and southern Canada to lay their eggs. No matter the time of year, coastal cormorants never fly far from land. They often perch on human-made structures like wood pilings, breakwaters and even partially sunken shipwrecks to plan their next fishing trip.

Cormorants, who are related to pelicans, are black and sleek and big (almost 3 feet or a meter long from the tip of their hooked beaks to their last tail feather). They also have fairly long curvy necks and webbed feet, which they use to propel themselves through the water. So if ever a bird was designed for underwater adventure, it's the cormorant. When they spot a fish, they dive in after it like a missile, and because they're such expert swimmers, they move like torpedoes under the surface. They can also sink like submarines: up to 100 feet or 30 meters below the waterline. When they catch what they're after, they bring it to the surface and swallow it whole, the head first.

In Asia, some fishermen use cormorants to catch fish. The birds catch the fish but they can't swallow them because the fishermen have put collars around their necks. Poor cormorants.

Those swans are called mute swans, and like the European starling and the house sparrow, they arrived here from across a different "pond"—what the British call the Atlantic Ocean. At one time, mute swans were held in such high regard in Britain that they were known as "birds royal" because it was only the king and a few favored subjects who were allowed to keep them. Later, when British settlers began arriving in North America, swans became a favorite status symbol of wealthy landowners who wanted to beautify their estates. They wanted the swans to remind them of home and to look pretty, which they most certainly do. With their porcelain-white plumage, their bright orange beaks and a big black knob directly below their eyes, they can enhance the look of any urban pond simply with their presence. (Trumpeter and tundra swans have smooth all-black beaks, although the tundra has a small yellow patch right in front of his eye.)

The reason they're called mute swans is that they rarely have much to say, except when they're angry. Then they're not at all shy about raising a ruckus. A mute swan's hiss can be as intimidating as a snake's, and they have a fairly nasty peck too. The sight of a swan chasing angrily after someone can be shocking, as that's not how we picture swans. (Though maybe we should, given that a swan's wing is powerful enough to break a man's arm!) We prefer to think of them as a snow-white centerpiece gliding gracefully, even regally, from one end of a pond to another.

Because mute swans aren't native to North America, when they arrived here, they couldn't migrate normally. Nor did their owners wish them to—not after all the trouble they took bringing them from England. But how

do you keep a winged creature from flying away? You clip its wings. So that's what many gamekeepers did—and continue to do today. This way, ornamental mute swans remain on city park ponds for visitors to enjoy. Ducks, geese, songbirds and raptors may come and go as they please, but not mute swans.

Does this mean they're still wild animals, or are they more like cats: wild at heart, but not much else? It's a question you may have a hard time answering.

Yet today not all mute swans suffer the same fate. More and more cygnets (swan chicks) manage to escape the gamekeeper's clippers and grow up intact, so when they're old enough, they too can leave the nest. As a result, there are now many populations of feral (a word meaning "once tame, now wild") mute swans breeding without the interference of human beings. Meanwhile, the swans left behind can take consolation from knowing that most park visitors love them and are happy to throw them fistfuls of dinner.

TOP: Brown pelicans are among the many seabirds California residents—including those in San Francisco—are familiar with.

BOTTOM: Cormorants have long sleek necks and slippery bodies—the better to fish with. They're also frequent visitors to city shores. LAURA COX

Chapter Six

Shells, Scales and Slime— Reptiles and Amphibians

There are two good reasons you don't see many snakes, turtles, lizards or frogs in Seattle, St. Louis or Saskatoon. The first is that all three are located in the northern half of North America (this is particularly true of Saskatoon), and reptiles and amphibians prefer to live farther south where it's warm (more about that later). The second is that all three are cities, and reptiles and amphibians don't do well in cities. Especially big ones. So you won't find many in Montreal, Minneapolis/ St. Paul or Manhattan either. You might come across a few here and there by a pond, in someone's compost or under a rock. But for the most part, snakes, turtles, lizards and frogs have a hard time fitting into cities the way raccoons and pigeons do. For them, trying to survive in what little green space is left among a city's girders and glass is a challenge few are prepared to meet.

Yes, people in cities do keep reptiles and amphibians as pets, but that's another kettle of fish entirely. (It's also a big mistake,

OPPOSITE: Frogs and other amphibians are reluctant city dwellers, but providing there's water, food and protection for them, even they can make a go of urban living. KATHY LAMB

ABOVE: Turtle Pond in New York City's Central Park is a place set aside especially for turtles and other small reptiles and amphibians living in America's biggest city. COLIN MILLS

OPPOSITE TOP: Eastern bullfrogs were brought to the Pacific Northwest decades ago as part of a harebrained scheme to produce frogs' legs. The scheme went nowhere, but the frogs went everywhere. VANCOUVER SUN

OPPOSITE BOTTOM: Red-eared slider turtles like this one are often bought as pets and then let go in the wild when they get too big and messy. That can wreak havoc on native turtle populations. LAURA COX

because reptiles and amphibians require special care few people can provide.) Wild reptiles and amphibians need wild places where human footprints haven't tread—or at least have tread lightly—and in cities those are few and far between. So when you're lucky enough to see a painted turtle sunning himself on a spray of lily pads in a downtown pond, or a garter snake slipping silently under a backyard fence, it's usually in spite of people, not because of them.

When people allow nature to exist within a city's limits, nature does assert herself enough to permit wildlife, even reptiles, to survive. The more green space there is in a city, the more city critters there are. But how much green space there is varies from city to city, which is why the number of reptiles and amphibians you'll find in cities varies too.

In the biggest city of all, New York City, there is a place where a number of turtle species live among some of the most expensive real estate in the world. It's called Turtle Pond and it lies at the base of Belvedere Castle in Central Park. In addition to turtles, several fish, frog and dragonfly species live in or around Turtle Pond, making it quite the urban oasis. Unfortunately, most of the turtles in Turtle Pond aren't really wild. Most were pets discarded by people too lazy or cruel to look after them. Chief among them is the red-eared slider turtle, a species native to the US South, but available in pet shops throughout North America, including Manhattan's. People buy red-eared sliders when they're small, not much bigger than a silver dollar, and toss them when they grow larger. An adult's shell is the size of a dinner plate, and when they're that big, they're not as appealing as they were as babies. They're harder to look after too.

Not only that, red-eared sliders can live up to forty years— much longer than most people are prepared to care for a pet—so they get pitched. The problem is that when they're set free in places like Turtle Pond, they compete with native turtles for nesting sites and food sources, and push those species away. Even worse, they can spread disease among native populations that kill them. This is called **displacement** and is an issue wherever red-eared sliders are sold.

So if you do find turtles in a park near where you live, there's a good chance that instead of painted or box or mud turtles—turtles who should be common to large parts of the United States and Canada—they'll be red-eared sliders. You can identify them by their dark green shells, yellow and green stripy heads and vivid red ovals behind their eyes. If there is a bright spot in this otherwise sad story, it's that there are still places in North American cities where turtles can live. Too bad they're usually the wrong sort of turtles.

ABOVE: Frogs the world over are disappearing, but scientists aren't sure why. It could be because their skin is so permeable to poisons and pollutants. LAURA COX

One of the biggest differences between animals like us and reptiles or amphibians is that reptiles and amphibians are **cold-blooded**, meaning their body temperatures are regulated by how warm or cold it is outside. If it's chilly, snakes, lizards and toads will be chilly too; if it's toasty warm, they'll be comfy and cozy. This isn't true of mammals and birds, who are warm-blooded. As long as conditions outside aren't too extreme, our body temperature stays the same (98.6 degrees Fahrenheit or 37 degrees Celsius in a healthy human being). This allows us to live fairly comfortably in a variety of climates, and helps explain how people manage to survive in every corner of the globe.

In contrast, reptiles and amphibians have to move around constantly to avoid getting too hot or too cold. When the sun is strong, snakes and lizards warm themselves on rocks, like sun worshippers at the beach. But when the sun retreats and it gets cold again, reptiles retreat too, to hiding places underground. In many parts of the United States and Canada winter is bitter; snow covers the ground for months. That makes life tough for reptiles and amphibians because, to survive, they have to find places between rock crevices, in the holes of trees, among leaf piles or under the ground to hibernate until spring. In the southern half of the continent, reptiles and amphibians still hibernate, but because it's so much warmer, they don't have to dig as far down to find suitable spots. Life is easier, which is why the south is where most urban—and rural—reptiles and amphibians tend to be.

But even for them city life is challenging simply because snakes, lizards and salamanders aren't suited to urban living. There are seven reasons why:

1. No matter the temperature, snakes, lizards, turtles and frogs can't dig through city tar and concrete to find underground places to hibernate—what scientists call "hibernacula." And if they can't hibernate, they can't survive.

2. Even if they can find a hibernaculum, they can't reproduce if they can't lay their eggs on soft ground—sandy, gravelly or grassy ground where their nests will be safe from predators like birds, skunks and raccoons. And how much soft ground is there in a city?

3. Many reptiles and amphibians wear camouflage to protect themselves, but camouflage works only if it mimics an animal's natural surroundings. And how many frogs do you know who can disguise themselves as a fast-food restaurant or a gas station?

4. Even if there are trees around for a tree frog to blend into, what protection will its tree-green color afford it against cars? Cars are ruthless killers of animals, especially animals who travel low to the ground.

5. Frogs are particularly susceptible to poison; it seeps right through their skin and into their organs. This means any weed or slug killer put down in urban gardens is likely to kill frogs, toads and salamanders.

6. Many people are afraid of reptiles, especially snakes, so they kill them indiscriminately (even though snakes have many more reasons to be afraid of people than the other way around).

7. All amphibians and some reptiles, including most turtles, need water to live—ponds, lakes, marshes and streams. And unless city planners include natural water features in their visions for Milwaukee or Montreal, there won't be any places for reptiles and amphibians to go.

Why are frogs Disappearing?

Some scientists believe as many as one-third of the world's 6,317 known species of frogs are on the edge of extinction, and they've advanced a number of explanations: destruction of wetlands, the places where frogs breed (in the United States more than 5 million acres [2 million hectares] of wetlands have been destroyed by development and industry); climate change; and declining water quality (a frog's skin is permeable, meaning it can absorb chemicals and gases right through to its organs; so if the water in which the frog lives is polluted, it could poison the frog). All or some of these factors may play a part in placing new stresses on frogs and the environments where they live. Or it could be something else entirely. At this point, scientists simply don't know.

ABOVE: Rattlesnakes live throughout the southwestern United States and will turn up in cities like Phoenix, Tucson and Albuquerque. J. FARLEY, US FISH AND WILDLIFE SERVICE

What's the difference between a frog and a toad?

Actually, there is no difference because toads are frogs. But when we think of frogs, we generally think of creatures with two bulging eyes, strong long legs, webbed hind feet and smooth slimy skin. When we think of toads, we think of creatures with short hind legs, warty dry skin, and poison glands behind the eyes. Also, while frogs lay clusters of eggs, toads lay eggs in long chains. The main difference is that toads spend most of their time on land, and frogs spend most of their time in or near water. So if you come across what looks like a toad or a frog in your flower bed, it's probably a toad.

ABOVE: Pacific tree frogs normally live in forest ponds, but urban living has presented them with all kinds of new challenges. MARY WATTS

With that much working against them, is it any wonder city life is no picnic for your average snake, frog or toad?

Yet the situation isn't all bad. The city-versus-snake (or turtle or frog) dilemma isn't without solutions—rare though they may be. For example, a good number of North American cities do have ponds, marshes and streams where reptiles and amphibians can live. In Milwaukee, there are several urban ponds and lagoons where, if you look closely, you can see painted or snapping turtles among the mud-colored leaves on the pond or lagoon floor. And in Montreal, several species of native turtles and snakes—mainly garter and northern brown snakes—live in suburban gardens, the next best thing to wilderness. The fact that Montreal sits on an island in the St. Lawrence River is also beneficial because it means there are places along the island's perimeter suitable for nests.

Those tidal marshes near Philadelphia and Washington, DC, mentioned in Chapter Three, are also havens for scaly critters. The Elizabeth Hartwell Mason Neck National Wildlife Refuge near Washington is home to 7 species of turtles; 4 species of lizards; 12 species of salamanders, frogs and toads; and 12 species of snakes. In the John Heinz National Wildlife Refuge near Philadelphia, there are 8 turtle, 3 snake, 2 toad and 6 frog species.

And even though Seattle may not be a place where large numbers of reptiles and amphibians skim and skitter, a few manage to cling on. Among the red-eared sliders who have taken over that city's urban wetlands are a number of native western painted turtles. Frogs can be found there as well, including (unfortunately) eastern bullfrogs, an invasive species as big as a boxing glove and just as in-your-face.

These dark green bug-eyed beasts have made themselves at home throughout Seattle's remaining wetlands, thanks to a foolhardy plan hatched decades ago to harvest their legs.

Frogs' legs, or *cuisses de grenouille* in French, were considered a great delicacy once, so people thought they'd make money from cultivating the frogs and serving their legs cooked and buttered (who knows what they did with the rest of the frog's body!). But like most get-rich-quick schemes, this one came to nothing—at least where the farmers were concerned. For the frogs, it was a jackpot because it meant they could go forth and multiply in an environment where they were literally the biggest frogs in the pond. And because of their voracious appetites, they wreaked havoc on many species of US Pacific Northwest and southern British Columbia wildlife. Eastern bullfrogs will swallow anything that fits their mouths. Ducklings, goslings and songbirds aren't safe; neither are mice, voles, snakes and other frogs, even smaller bullfrogs.

Yet despite living next door to such bullies, some native Pacific tree frogs have held their own in Seattle and elsewhere. And if you're really lucky, you may even find an extremely rare northern alligator lizard (don't worry, they're only about 8 inches or 20 centimeters long) or a blue-bellied western fence lizard sunning themselves in the city's forested lands.

Even in Toronto, Canada's largest city, five native species of turtles survive in some city parks. They include the now very rare Blanding's turtle, which aboriginal people call "the turtle with the sun under its chin" because of its bright yellow throat and chin, and the stinkpot turtle, so named because it releases a foul-smelling fluid when it's picked up by a predator. Six snake and nine frog species (including the so-called spring peeper, which emits a peep-like croak early in April) also call the city home because of the green spaces that remain. The number of human Torontonians (more than 5 million) also has been a boon to some snakes, because human garbage attracts rats,

TOP: If snakes manage to survive in cities, it's in spite of people not because of them. LAURA COX

BOTTOM: One of the reasons snakes, including garter snakes, are in such peril in cities is that people are afraid of them and will hurt them deliberately. WAYNE CAMPBELL

◎ What are the biggest reptiles in North America?

American alligators and crocodiles are by far the biggest reptiles in North America. The former are found throughout Florida and several southeastern US states, while the latter are found only on the southernmost tip of Florida. Crocodiles are far more secretive than alligators; have pointier, more triangular mouths; and live in salt water rather than fresh.

The longest snake in North America is the highly endangered indigo snake, which can grow to just under 9 feet (3 meters) in length. In 2003 one was photographed slithering across a roadway inside the Kennedy Space Center in Florida. Chances are it came from the nearby Merritt Island National Wildlife Refuge in Cape Canaveral.

and snakes eat rats. Railway and power lines can be inadvertent blessings to them as well, because they create travel corridors.

Regardless of where they live—in Seattle, Toronto or Turtle Pond—what all these reptiles and amphibians have in common is that they're small to modest in size. Garter snakes grow to about 3 feet (1 meter) long; the painted turtle has a shell about 10 inches (25 centimeters) in diameter; and a tree frog is no more than 2 inches (5 centimeters) from nose to rump. The reason for their small size is that they all live in the north where it's difficult to keep a cold-blooded body warm.

One of nature's constants is that animals only grow as large as they need to be, because the bigger they are, the more energy they need to sustain themselves. Consequently in the northern United States and Canada, where keeping warm requires a great deal of energy, it doesn't make sense for reptiles to grow big. In the south this isn't the case. Throughout the southern United States, where it is warm, reptiles do grow bigger—as big as alligators, who live throughout Florida and in parts of Louisiana, Georgia, Mississippi, Alabama and Texas too. In these places reptiles and amphibians don't have to worry about freezing to death, so they can devote more energy to growing.

Which is why if you travel to Florida, you'd better be prepared to share the state with more than a million American alligators. (For some people, that's more than a million reasons never to go.) This wasn't true fifty years ago when Florida's alligators were on the verge of extinction. Most people had no use for them except as shoes or handbags. But others thought alligators were worth saving, so they pressed the Florida government to take action—which it did. Gradually, between

1962 and 1988, officials made hunting alligators in the entire state illegal. They hoped that by doing so, the few alligators left would have a chance.

No one guessed at the time how much of a chance. Thanks to that ban, Florida alligators made such a comeback that new laws had to be written to allow intermittent hunting to keep the animal's skyrocketing numbers in check. Today, the alligator is Florida's state reptile, and no matter where you go in the Sunshine State's sixty-seven counties, there's a good chance you'll see one—or two or three.

You'll see them elsewhere in the south too, as long as it's warm and there's sufficient water. Even in Houston (America's fourth-largest city), you might see the odd alligator in one of that Texas metropolis's creeks, lakes or bayous. That's how adjusted to urban living they've become. Not long ago, one was caught swimming in a Houston community swimming pool, while another was hit by a car while trying to cross Memorial Drive,

ABOVE: If you're afraid of alligators, you don't want to live in Florida, where there are more than a million of them. TIM DONOVAN/FLORIDA FISH AND WILDLIFE COMMISSION

Amazing Animal Adaptation

Floridians are used to alligators. With more than a million in the state, they have to be. But in the YMCA? One Friday a couple of years ago a woman plunged into a Cocoa Beach YMCA pool only to wonder if that four-foot-long visitor lying along the bottom really was what she thought it was. Her guess was confirmed moments later by the pool's lifeguard, Tim Phiopot, who had to restrain a second swimmer from joining her.

"She [the second woman] goes, 'That's not a gator,'" Phiopot told television station WFTV after the event. "We kept walking and, sure enough, she goes, 'Oh my god, that's a gator!'"

Trappers were brought in to deal with the situation, but not before the original swimmer—ironically wearing an anti-Gators-football-team T-shirt—was rescued. Fittingly, her allegiance belonged to the Auburn University Tigers, who were due to play the University of Florida's Gators the following day.

How the alligator got into the pool was for the animal to know and YMCA officials to figure out, but it's safe to assume he used one of a system of pipes leading from the ground into the building. After all, to an alligator, one waterway is like another. That's the essence of urban animal adaptations. Who cares who or what built it, as long as it works!

ABOVE: Florida alligators have been known to turn up in urban swimming pools, but for the most part they know enough to stay away from people.
TIM DONOVAN/FLORIDA FISH AND WILDLIFE COMMISSION

one of the main thoroughfares bisecting west Houston.

But it's in Florida where alligators are as much a part of the landscape as golf courses—which is where they're often found. (This is particularly true of courses with water features, so be careful when you look for a missing ball!) The longest gator ever recorded was 14 feet, 7.5 inches (4.4 meters), and the heaviest was 1,043 pounds (473 kilograms), though lengths of 10 feet (3 meters) are typical. Nevertheless, as ferocious as alligators appear, and as intimidating as they can be, Floridians have learned to live with them, which is really only fair since alligators were there first. (The alligator's oldest ancestors are thought to have lived 150 million years ago, at the same time as dinosaurs.)

Today alligators and Floridians are so adept at do-si-doing around each other that, according to the Florida Fish and Wildlife Conservation Commission, encounters are exceptions rather than the rule. Occasionally officials do hear of an unsettling collision between a canoeist paddling one of the hundreds of canals that crisscross the state and a gator out for a swim. Perhaps the canoeist failed to realize that what looked like a log was really a scaly prehistoric reptile with up to eighty teeth arrayed over two sets of massive jaws. There are also times when alligators make their way into swimming pools. (Not exactly the kind of guest most people would like to find dipping and diving in the deep end.)

However, if an alligator does misbehave in an urban area, conservation officials will take steps. Sadly, about 15,000 alligators are killed each year for being what state officials call "nuisances." Drains and culverts are favorite gator hangouts.

Yet for the most part, such rendezvous are rare because people and gators know that the best—really the *only*—way to get along is to avoid each other. As one Florida conservation officer put it: "Most alligators got big because they learned to stay away from people."

A similar truce has been worked out between people in the US southeast and the large, and occasionally venomous, snakes adapted to the hot, sultry climate of Louisiana, Alabama and Mississippi. Snakes such as the cottonmouth water moccasin, a semi-aquatic viper who isn't afraid of much, have been known to fall out of trees directly in the paths of people (how loud can you scream?). Happily, it's not a daily occurrence, but if you live in the US southeast and don't want snakes in your backyard, be sure to cut your grass short. That way they can't hide in it.

On the other side of the country much the same kind of understanding has been reached between residents of Phoenix and Tucson and the many rattlesnakes living in those Arizona cities' desert parks. Thirteen rattlesnake species are native to Arizona, southern New Mexico and southeastern California, including the western diamondback, the 7-foot (2.1-meter) namesake of the Arizona Diamondbacks, Phoenix's professional baseball team. There are seven city wildlife preserves in Phoenix, America's fifth-largest city, including the sprawling 16,000-acre (6,500-hectare) South Mountain Park, a breathtaking mountain wilderness of rocks, sand, cacti and grass that Arizonans claim is the largest city park in the United States. And rattlesnakes live in all seven.

If problems do arise, they're due to the inability of rattlesnakes (not that we should blame them) to tell where wildlife preserves end and city streets begin. Thus it's not uncommon to

ABOVE: Invasive species like this Burmese python snaking its way across a Florida highway do terrible damage to native flora and fauna. MELISSA FARLOW/ NATIONAL GEOGRAPHIC

How many exotic animals are brought into North America each year?

No one knows for sure, but, sadly, it's a growing trade. Between 1992 and 2002, the most recent years for which government statistics are available, the trade in wildlife and wildlife products to the United States jumped by 62 percent, and the number of different species bought and sold increased 75 percent. In 2002, 38,000 live mammals, 365,000 live birds, 2 million live reptiles, 49 million live amphibians and 216 million live fish were imported into the United States. In 2010, the US Association of Reptile Keepers said there were 2 million pet pythons across the country. Ninety percent of wild-caught reptiles are said to die in their first year of captivity either because of physical trauma suffered during capture or because of an owner's inability to look after them properly. The US Centers for Disease Control estimates that 74,000 people come down with salmonella each year as a result of coming into contact with pet reptiles and amphibians.

find rattlers in any number of Phoenix backyards, sunning themselves on a warm spring day. Snakes don't really hear things; instead, they detect vibrations in the ground. So when they detect the vibration of human footsteps, they usually hightail it out of the person's way. But sometimes, if a snake is asleep, the vibrations go unnoticed until the snake can no longer help waking up to the sight of a wide-eyed, horrified, possibly shouting homeowner. What happens next will depend on the actors. The homeowner may get bitten; the snake may get killed; or, best scenario of all, the two will part company and agree never to cross paths again. Similar encounters can also occur on Phoenix golf courses or when Phoenicians (what people who live in Phoenix call themselves) go for a hike. That's why they're always careful to wear sturdy high-topped boots!

But when it comes to reptiles, it's not just snakes who call desert cities home. Lizards do too, including the stout-bodied, black-and-orange, 2-foot (0.6-meter) Gila monster. They can be observed sometimes hunting or lying in the sun on the fringes of Phoenix or Tucson wildlife parks where soft desert edges meet hard city roads. Though Gila monsters are mainly nocturnal and spend most of their time underground out of the blazing desert sun, they may appear in spring when there are nesting birds and small reptiles to eat.

Thanks to global warming, however, such appearances could become more and more rare. Scientists have found that as the world gets hotter, lizards are spending less time in the sun and more in the shade. That's troubling, because the more time they spend hiding, the less they devote to eating and mating, activities essential to their survival. So serious is the problem that scientists say if the world continues to warm at its current rate of 0.04 degrees Fahrenheit (0.02 degrees Celsius) a year, 20 percent of all the world's lizards could vanish by 2080. And if you wonder how that would affect you, consider how many insects lizards eat. With fewer lizards around, the world could be a much buggier place.

We have already talked in this chapter about how red-eared slider turtles and eastern bullfrogs cause problems for native species. But when it comes to invasive reptiles and amphibians in North America, they're just the tip of the tail. There's no limit to the number of scaly and/or slimy creatures people are prepared to dump in places they don't belong. To appreciate how bad the situation is, you need only return to Florida, where up to 150,000 Burmese pythons—snakes that grow up to 23 feet (7 meters) long—have been allowed to breed unfettered in the Everglades. Burmese pythons are native to Southeast Asia, not Florida, but commercial pet traders imported them into North America for people who thought it would be "cool" to keep a snake in the house. There's nothing cool about it. Exotic animals don't belong in houses or apartments, and they often get dumped in city parks or wilderness areas. Drop a Burmese python into Chicago's Grant Park, and it'll freeze to death over winter. (That is, if police don't catch it first.) Drop one in the Everglades and you'll contribute to what has become a statewide crisis in which even alligators aren't safe.

The problem arose in 1992 when Hurricane Andrew set free hundreds of pythons from local pet shops and breeders' basements. The result was a second storm of a very different but equally destructive nature. In a place without natural predators, the pythons multiplied to a catastrophic degree by eating

TOP: Geckos, like this red one, are among the most common of urban lizards. They can often be found skittering up walls and along ceilings in hot places. LAURA COX

BOTTOM: North America is home to a number of native turtles, but too often they're pushed out of their natural habitats by discarded red-eared slider turtles like this one. LAURA COX

the local wildlife—everything from squirrels to possums to lizards. They've even been known to challenge alligators. After attempting to eat a particularly large gator, one snake exploded.

The crisis became so serious that in 2009 a 12-foot (3.5-meter) snake killed a two-year-old girl when it slithered into her crib in the small town of Oxford, about 50 miles (80 kilometers) northwest of Orlando. The same year a freakishly cold winter gripped the state, so about half the pythons froze to death. Florida residents reported seeing them falling out of trees (which made a change from spotting them in swimming pools). But thousands remain. Recently Florida wildlife officials and sport hunters have been given permits to kill the snakes en masse, and the state has finally banned their sale. Yet reptile clubs continue to object, which goes to show how stubborn some people can be.

BELOW: Northwestern garter snakes can grow to 3 feet (1 meter) long. That's as big as reptiles get in the cold north. They grow much bigger in the south where it's warm. WANDA UNDERHILL

The Burmese python is possibly the most extreme example of how an invasive species can help destroy an environment, but Florida is home to all sorts of other alien species too. Caimans (a smaller kind of crocodile), boa constrictors and green iguanas are also established there, along with numerous other smaller, but equally out-of-place, snakes and lizards who also do considerable damage. The iguana, a large lizard native to Mexico and Central America, has taken to basking on sidewalks, docks, seawalls and lawns. They usually stay clear of people, but they pose a big threat to pets and gardens. Altogether, more than two thousand species of alien plants and animals have been identified in Florida, and more are coming to light all the time. Small wonder the problem costs the US government more than $138 billion a year.

All this goes to show what a colossal impact— both deliberate and accidental—we have on reptiles and amphibians simply by living where we live and doing what we do. A Burmese python or green iguana feasting on Florida's native fauna—and wrecking the environment in the process—can thank the state's upright, two-legged creatures for that privilege. If it weren't for people, they'd never be in Florida—and Florida would be better off. At least a midland painted turtle in Toronto's Rouge Park can derive some satisfaction from knowing that southeastern Ontario, with all its traffic fumes and construction din, really is home. But as in Florida, the turtle's fate rests in the hands of people. Will they continue to set aside green space for midland painted turtles and other fragile reptiles and amphibians, or will they allow that green space to be paved over for parking? The only difference is that in Ontario the people making these decisions wear Gore-Tex and faux fur instead of floral prints and sandals.

TOP: One of the reasons snakes can live in cities is that they eat rats. And cities are full of rats. BLAIR COX

BOTTOM: Frogs, like this one, are usually found in or near water. Sometimes people like to have them in their backyard ponds as decoration. BLAIR COX

Chapter Seven

The Creepy Crawlies— Insects and Spiders

Insects are everywhere. No matter where on Earth you are—a steamy South American jungle, a frozen Canadian pond or even Times Square in New York—insects are there too. Living in busy cities full of shopping malls, parking lots and shimmering glass towers, we may not appreciate that, but it's true. Tunneling under malls are armies of ants and beetles. Hovering over parking lots are squadrons of flies and mosquitoes. And slithering through the drains of shimmering glass towers are units of silverfish. They're all insects, and despite the millions of dollars North Americans spend each year on bug spray, they cling on: flying, buzzing, hopping, hunting and reproducing. When you add spiders to the mix (spiders aren't insects; they only look like them) you can't help but realize that the world—even the urban world—is one buggy place. They are, hands down, the most successful and widespread creatures in the whole animal kingdom.

So when it comes to identifying North America's most successful *urban* critters, insects don't take a backseat to

OPPOSITE: *"'Will you walk into my parlor?' said the Spider to the Fly."* You don't have to think twice about how that visit ended. Spiders and flies are among the most numerous of all city critters. CATHY KEIFER/ DREAMSTIME.COM

ABOVE: After butterflies, lady beetles are probably the most beloved of all urban insects because they eat so many garden pests. DOREEN GRAY

anyone—even people. Yet, because humans leave such a heavy footprint wherever we tread, even insects aren't immune. As with every other kind of creature, it depends on what kind of insect they are. Sometimes they benefit from the things we do; sometimes they don't.

The only reason silverfish reside in pipes is that they find food there. Termites in the US South eat dead wood, and in a city like Dallas or Mobile, what better source is there than a rotting house? (Ditto for carpenter ants up north.) When rain is allowed to pool in buckets, flowerpot basins, plastic toys, trashcans, recycling containers, wading pools or any of a dozen other receptacles people leave lying around, it can become a breeding pond for flies and mosquitoes.

At the same time, many other insect species can't adapt to urban settings, and suffer for it. Bees and butterflies ingest nectar from flowering plants, so when urban gardens and vacant lots give way to strip malls and parking lots, bees and butterflies simply give way.

Even so, hundreds of thousands of different insect species continue to fill North American soils and skies. They are among the million or more species entomologists (scientists who study insects) have identified globally. With so many different types of insects creeping and crawling over our globe, naming and categorizing them is challenging. There is always an exception to test every rule. Nevertheless, most insects belong to one of five main insect groups: beetles, flies, wasps (this group also includes bees and ants), bugs (the common name for crawling insects), and butterflies and moths. Thus, within any North American city you can name, you can expect to find insects representing each of these five basic categories.

Beetles are the most common. There are more than 300,000 different types in the world, and many live in North America. So if you've seen one beetle, you definitely haven't seen them all. Some are minuscule, far too small to see with the naked eye.

Others are enormous. The goliath beetle, a black-and-gold monster from Africa, is as big around as an Olympic medal and as heavy as an apricot. And in between are tens of thousands of other beetles the size of pinheads, pennies, pimples and more. They can be bright as balloons—red, blue, green, orange, yellow, purple, pewter or bronze—or plain black or white. They can be striped, spotted or both. Whatever your design taste, there's probably a beetle somewhere in the world to suit it.

How common a beetle is in a city depends on how adaptable that beetle is to city living. (That should be a familiar refrain by now.) The carpet beetle, a round or oval-shaped, multi-colored insect with tufts of bristles on its abdomen, feels perfectly at home in a human house because it feeds on dry skin, hair from humans and pets, and dead insects. That makes the carpet beetle as efficient as any vacuum cleaner and about as common too. Then there's the beer beetle, a shiny red, yellow or orange insect named for its fondness for alcohol, usually the kind that occurs in fermenting fruit. But that's not to say it's averse to other kinds as well. So if you happen to notice a brightly colored beetle turning a belly flop into your dad's glass of lager, chances are it's a (very happy) urban beer beetle.

Other kinds of beetles fit well into urban living too, but the most popular of all is the lady beetle, or as it's also known, the ladybug or ladybird. They're even thought to be lucky. If one lands on your shoulder, superstition says you should leave it there or you'll thwart the magic. People interested in organic gardening are so fond of these bright red, orange or pink spotted beetles that they'll buy packages of them to set free. Why? Because they eat so many garden pests. So beloved is the seven-spotted lady beetle—one of more than 500 lady beetle species in North America, and named for the seven discrete

What defines an insect?

All insects, regardless of species, share certain characteristics. They include an external skeleton, or **exoskeleton**, multiple eyes (sometimes hundreds of them), six legs and three basic body parts: the head, thorax and abdomen. An insect's head does what yours does—scouts out its environment and ingests food. The thorax is the insect's transportation center, the part that anchors its six legs and wings. The abdomen contains the insect's digestive and reproductive organs. In bees and wasps, the abdomen is also where you'll find the stinger, since a stinger is essentially a modified egg-laying tube.

ABOVE: Lady beetles are also known as ladybugs and ladybirds. They were named in medieval times after Mary, "Our Lady." CATHERINE BELL

TOP: Mosquitoes are among the most common and irritating of all urban flying insects. Females need the blood of animals, including humans, to nourish their young. VANCOUVER SUN

BOTTOM: Butterflies are disappearing from many urban landscapes, but several species of swallowtails still turn up each summer in many urban gardens. LAURA COX

black spots on its orangey red shell—that the states of Delaware, Massachusetts, Tennessee, Ohio, New Hampshire and Pennsylvania have declared it their official insect.

Seldom is an insect the object of so much human affection (only butterflies conjure similar feelings), but the love affair with the lady beetle goes all the way back to medieval times. The beetle's red wings reminded Catholics of "Our Lady," the Virgin Mary, because of the red cloak she often wore in paintings at that time. And when a group of medieval French farmers prayed to "Our Lady" to rid their fields of pests, she sent lady beetles to eat them. The farmers regarded the seven spots on the lady beetle's back as emblematic of Mary's—Our Lady's—joys and sorrows. That's how the lady beetle got its name. And yes, in case you were wondering, male lady beetles are called lady beetles too. Even the pink ones.

Flies, the second common insect group, are distinctive for having two wings. Other kinds of flying insects, including butterflies and dragonflies, have four, so they're not true flies, despite their names. True flies like houseflies, fruit flies and mosquitoes also have large compound eyes and claws or pads on their feet that enable them to walk up walls and along ceilings without falling off. There are thought to be about 25,000 different kinds of flies in North America, but there could be more. We don't know because they aren't studied as much as beetles. Even so, in the northern half of North America—from the middle of the United States to the most northernmost point of Canada—there are more species of flies than any other living creature. That won't come as a surprise to anyone who's hiked the Canadian woods in summer. In June, July and August, northern forests are engulfed by black flies and mosquitoes—so many that it's like walking through clouds of them.

The best-known urban fly is the common housefly, because it lives where people do. Historically, it was for the most disgusting of reasons: because it breeds in animal (including human) dung. Today in our modern and comparatively clean cities, it uses garbage or compost instead. The resulting larvae, called maggots or grubs, are grayish white turd-shaped insects who gorge themselves on the guts of dead animals or the excrement of live ones. One of the most remarkable things about flies is the hair on their feet, which they use to taste what they land on. How revolting is that?

Dirty and annoying as houseflies can be, at least they don't bite. The same can't be said for other urban flies. Mosquitoes—the bane of so many North American summers, particularly in plains or prairie cities like Fargo and Winnipeg—are relentless biters. At least the females are. Males feed exclusively on plant nectar and only live a week—just long enough to mate. Females feed on nectar too, but they need animal blood to develop and lay eggs, which takes three to five days. Even then

ABOVE: Dragonflies aren't considered true flies because they have four wings, not two. LAURA COX

BELOW: Though not as numerous as other kinds of urban insects, dragonflies are certainly among the most eye-catching. ELSPETH ANDERSON

TOP: Honeybees aren't native to North America. They were imported from Europe in the seventeenth century. But they've since become an essential part of North American agriculture. TESS VAN DONKELAAR

BOTTOM: Yellow jackets, the plague of countless urban picnics, live in paperlike nests like this one that are often found in the eaves of houses. REBEKAH MAITLAND

they're not done "bugging" people, because once they've laid their first set of eggs, they'll hunt for more blood to feed a second set. Mosquitoes only have to mate once to lay two sets of eggs.

Another familiar biting fly, at least in cities by the sea, is the sand fly, or, as it's also known, the biting midge, the punky or the no-see-um, thanks to its ability to bite and not be seen. In fact, in some ways sand flies are even peskier than mosquitoes because they're smaller, so they can fly through the mesh screens people put up in windows and doors.

Fleas, another kind of biting insect, aren't flies. They belong to a separate insect order called Siphonaptera. But, boy, can they bite—dogs, cats and people. And since cities are full of dogs, cats and people, cities are full of fleas too. A single flea is no bigger than a pencil tip, but they can be giant-sized headaches because of how difficult they are to get rid of. They're armored so heavily with disclike body plates—like little stegosauruses or tiny Arthurian knights—that they're almost impossible to squish. Fleas bite because, like mosquitoes, they need animal blood to live.

They get it by puncturing an animal's—including a human animal's—skin and sucking the blood below. A flea's head has two bladelike structures sticking out of it that the flea uses to tear its victim's skin. Then it injects saliva into the victim's blood to keep it from clotting. It's this saliva that makes fleabites so itchy. Without it, we probably wouldn't notice them.

Bees, which are part of the third main insect group (along with wasps and ants), are also flying insects, but they get their nourishment from plants. There are bumblebees, honeybees and digger bees.

Many bumblebee species are native to North America and exist throughout the continent. Though the more the continent gets paved over, the fewer of these fuzzy, buzzy and mainly harmless (unless you're allergic or happen to step on one) yellow-and-black insects there are. Bumblebees are most common in summer when they forage for flower nectar and pollen. Plants depend on bees to carry pollen from one plant to another. Without them, they wouldn't be able to reproduce.

Honeybees are not native to North America. Like pigeons, they were brought here from Europe in the seventeenth century. Since then they've become an essential part of North American agriculture because they're used to pollinate so many different kinds of commercial crops. Each spring, hives of honeybees are trucked all over the continent like fertilizer. They go from place to place—field to field—according to the time of year and the crop. When they're delivered to a certain field, they're set free to pollinate whatever is growing there—corn, hops, alfalfa, fruit trees, you name it. Then when they're done, they're rounded up and transported to where they're needed next. It's another example of how humankind manipulates nature to serve industry.

People who keep bees in cities—and many North American cities, including New York, Los Angeles,

TOP: On a summer's day, you never know what kind of insect might turn up knocking on your gate. A dragonfly for instance. MICHAEL A. GATTO

BOTTOM: Bumblebees are frequent summertime visitors to urban parks and gardens. They often buzz around the clover in lawns, drawing nectar from its flowers, so be careful not to step on one. REBEKAH MAITLAND

ABOVE: Butterflies need urban gardens to survive. The fewer parks and gardens there are in cities, the fewer butterflies there'll be. LAURA COX

OPPOSITE: Earwigs got their name from the false belief that they crawl inside people's ears and breed in their brains. It's nothing but an old wives' tale, but the name has stuck. LAURA COX

Chicago, Seattle, San Francisco and Vancouver, encourage beekeeping—keep honeybees. In fact, honeybees are so important to North American food production that it's said this little sunflower-yellow insect is responsible for one of every three forkfuls of food you eat.

Recently, however, honeybees appear to have fallen on hard times. Evidence suggests their numbers have plummeted, and that's bad news for everyone. True, fewer honeybees would mean fewer stings, but when you think how integral honeybees are to almost everything we eat, the least we owe them is a place in an urban park. Several theories have been advanced to explain their apparent disappearance, including deadly radio waves and even terrorist plots. For a while scientists blamed a kind of mite that eats honeybees. They worried that these mites, called varroa, were becoming resistant to insecticides, and because of that were surviving long enough to attack honeybees like never before.

But now it looks as if climate change may be to blame. According to new research done at the University of Toronto, because flowers are blooming earlier than they used to, they're no longer in synch with bees and their rhythms. In other words, there may be just as many bees as there always were, but they're not around early enough in the season to do their job.

Digger bees is the common name given to a group of robust, fast-flying and ground-nesting bee with velvety fur. There are about 900 species in the United States and Canada, and like bumblebees and honeybees, digger bees play an important role in plant pollination. They're also known as longhorn bees because of the males' exceptionally long antennae.

When it comes to wasps, the most common and dangerous kind in North America is the yellow jacket, a little bullet of an insect with black tiger stripes and long orangey wings.

Yellow jackets build lanternlike nests out of saliva and wood fibers that hang under the eaves of houses, decks, porches and other human-made structures. These nests, which are home to wasp colonies, become a problem for people in late summer when the queen is dead and there are no more eggs to look after. When wasp eggs hatch in spring, the resulting larvae need insects to eat. So the nest's workers (all of them female) spend their days gathering insects to feed them. But when there are no more eggs or larvae left in the nest—when they've all grown up and abandoned it—worker wasps gather food for themselves instead. The problem is that they eat meat and food with sugar in it. That's why when you barbecue burgers or spill a bottle of soda, it's like signing a hand-engraved invitation to a swarm of yellow jackets—and their stingers.

Bugs, the fourth main insect category, is the common name given to any kind of crawling insect. These include nasty, pinpoint-sized bloodsuckers called bedbugs, which, like honeybees, were brought to North America from Europe hundreds of years ago. Now, like many human immigrants, bedbugs have made themselves comfortable here, but unlike human immigrants, they contribute nothing to our way of life except grief. Anyone unfortunate enough to share a bed with a host of bedbugs is liable to wake up covered in painful, itchy and long-lasting bites. Bedbugs are so tough and resilient that they can settle anywhere—from San Jose to St. John's and Kalamazoo to Calgary. They're a particular problem in hotel rooms because when people pack suitcases, they may accidentally pack bedbugs too. That's how they get around. But because bedbugs are so small, no one knows they're there…till they start biting.

Are earwigs and head lice insects?

Yes, but they don't fit neatly into any insect category. Lice are those nasty, hungry, wingless bloodsuckers that bite human scalps. The singular of lice is louse, which is where the word "lousy" comes from. No wonder. Earwigs, however, only sound gross. They get their name from an old but false belief that they crawl into people's ears and breed in their brains. They don't. But they're happy to scavenge around your kitchen for the odd piece of fruit or bread.

How can you tell a moth from a butterfly?

There's no real scientific distinction, but there are a few telltale differences: 1) butterflies are brighter in color than moths; 2) moths fly at night while butterflies fly during the day; 3) butterfly bodies tend to be slender and free of hair, while moth bodies are a little bulkier and more "hirsute" (a fancy word for hairy). Also, butterfly antennae end in a little swelling or club at the tip; moth antennae don't.

ABOVE: One of the ways to attract butterflies to your garden is to plant plants they like. There are all kinds of them, from buddleias to clover to zinnias. LAURA COX

There have always been fewer butterflies and moths than any other kind of insect. In North America there are only about 750 species. But because butterflies are so appealing to people, they get more attention than any other kind of bug. One of the loveliest sights in an urban garden is a butterfly fluttering delicately over a flower. They look as light and fragile as fairies. As a result, most of the insects on North American endangered species lists are butterflies.

Butterflies exhibit so many different patterns and colors on their wings that identifying different species takes real patience and study. Unfortunately, because big cities don't attract many butterflies anymore, it's comparatively easy to name the few that remain. One is the swallowtail. Members of this large butterfly family are common on every continent except Antarctica. In North America most swallowtails are yellow, but they can be orange, red and blue too. Regardless of their hue, they almost always have inky black stripes framing their wings—wings that form a point at the bottom like a swallow's tail. Hence their name. The Oregon swallowtail, a yellow-and-black butterfly whose wingspan can be as big as 4 inches (10 centimeters), is the state insect of Oregon. The eastern tiger swallowtail, an even bigger yellow-and-black butterfly, is the state insect of Virginia and the state butterfly of Georgia, Delaware and South Carolina.

Other butterflies well known to city dwellers include the cabbage white because of its appetite for vegetables urban gardeners grow, and the orange sulfur—a yellow/orange butterfly that feeds on nectar from dandelions, milkweed and asters. Orange sulfurs are present throughout the contiguous forty-eight US states and much of southern Canada, so if you happen to see an orange-winged butterfly flitting over a vacant lot strewn with yellow dandelions, it's probably an orange sulfur.

But perhaps the best known and most beloved of all North American butterflies is the monarch. Sadly, monarchs aren't as common as they once were either. Even so, if there's one butterfly that most people in North America recognize and have fond feelings for, it's this bright black-and-orange Mexican native who arrives here in late May or early June. So popular is the monarch that the US Congress once considered a bill that would have made it the US national insect. The Mexican government has proposed using it as a symbol of North American free trade.

One reason monarchs are so popular is that we can't help marveling at their migrations. Canadian and most US winters are too cold for monarchs, so they have to return to Mexico or southern California to hibernate. If the butterflies summer in Canada, that's a journey of more than 1,550 miles (2,500 kilometers). Actually most scientists believe monarchs lay eggs along the way, and that it's their offspring who complete the journey. But it's still an impressive feat.

Tragically, the Mexican forests where monarchs breed are being cut down at such a rate that fewer and fewer monarchs survive each year. Extreme weather fluctuations caused by climate change are taking a toll too. But efforts are being made to protect them. There's a sanctuary in the Pacific Grove district of Monterey, California, where monarchs overwinter from October to February. It's right next door to the (what else?) Butterfly Grove Inn. So popular are the butterflies that the sanctuary has to engage volunteers each year to explain their ecology to tourists.

Moths, the butterflies' less attractive cousins, usually come out at night. You can see them fluttering around porch lights or street lamps because they mistake these artificial lights for the

TOP: Though they look similar, moths and butterflies differ. Moths, like this one, have hair on them, tend to be duller in color and come out at night rather than the day. LAURA COX

BOTTOM: As a rule, people don't like moths as much as they like butterflies. Probably because moths get into our kitchens and eat our clothes. Butterflies don't. JUTTA SCHULZ

What are millipedes?

Like spiders, millipedes aren't insects, but they're small like insects with the same kind of exoskeletons. They differ in the number of legs they have. Insects have six; millipedes (as their name, which means "a thousand feet," suggests) have many more—anywhere from 50 to 150.

Cities are full of millipedes. Outside they live under rocks or logs or lawn turf, anywhere where it's moist, because they feed on rotting organic matter. But during the spring and fall they may invade people's houses, especially if there's been a lot of rain, as houses tend to be damp then too. When the houses dry up, the infestations end, because without moisture millipedes die.

Sowbugs or pillbugs are also common in cities. People tend to confuse them with millipedes, but they're actually land-dwelling relatives of the crab and shrimp, introduced to North America from Europe. Sometimes they're called "roly polys" because they curl up into little balls when they're threatened.

light of the moon, which they use to orient themselves. This is where the expression "like moths to a flame" comes from. Among the most common urban moths are those who eat clothes. In fact, there's a whole moth family called clothes moths. They display several different wing shapes and colors—both dark and light—and, depending on the species, range in size from 1/16 to 1 6/16 inches (0.7 to 3.6 centimeters). In other words, they're all pretty small. But whatever their size, they can do serious damage to your shirts, skirts and pants if they're made of natural fibers like wool, linen, fur or silk. Actually, it's the moth larvae who are to blame. They zero in on places stained with food, drinks, sweat or even urine, because all those substances provide caterpillars with nutrients they need to grow. In the old days, people used to put small white balls made with an insect repellent called camphor in their trunks to protect their clothes from moths. That's why when you open an old trunk, it often has a "mothball smell." Today, as long as you keep your clothing clean and aired, it ought to be okay. But if you find tiny holes in it one day, you'll know why.

Urban moths can also be found in bags of flour, cereal, nuts or pet food. So-called Indian meal moths (their wings are pale gray at the bottom and red-brown at the top) often find their way into bags of these nutrient-rich foods, with the result that your kitchen can become infested with them. Once again it's the meal moth larvae—the caterpillars—who actually eat the stuff. They're about half an inch (1.3 centimeters) long and dirty white in color.

Cities are full of spiders, too, but spiders aren't insects. They're often mistaken for them because they're about the same size and share some insect features, including an exoskeleton (a skeleton that wraps around the insect's or spider's organs) and very small bodies relative to their long legs. But they're fundamentally different. Spiders have no antennae, eight legs instead of six, and two distinct body parts, not three. And they spin webs; insects don't. In fact, the word *spider* comes from an old English word meaning "to spin."

What spiders need more than anything else to survive are insects to eat. All spiders are carnivorous, meaning they don't eat plants, but unlike other carnivores, they don't actually eat flesh. What they do is suck juices out of insects they paralyze with their venom, and live off that. You've probably heard that flies are a favorite spider food. In 1829 British poet Mary Howitt wrote a still-famous poem about the two that begins: "'Will you walk into my parlor?' said the Spider to the Fly." But spiders eat more than just flies. In fact, they'll eat almost anything that flies, leaps, crawls or scuttles, providing it's small enough to tackle and kill.

ABOVE: Spiders are not insects. They have eight legs, not six, and they spin webs. Insects don't. COLIN MILLS

BELOW: Spiders use their webs to trap insect prey. Then they paralyze them with their venom.
THOMAS LANGLANDS/DREAMSTIME.COM

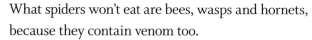

What are the world's deadliest spiders?

As with insects, it's impossible to say with real certainty what the deadliest spiders in the world are, but included among the candidates are these five: 1) the Australian Redback spider, whose venomous bite can lead to death if it goes untreated; 2) the tree-dwelling funnel-web spider, another Australian resident whose venom can damage a person's nervous system and lead to death; 3) the Brazilian wandering spider, a South American jungle spider that sometimes hides in banana crates when they're shipped from one country to another, and whose venom, like the Australian spiders', is harmful to a person's nervous system; 4) the brown recluse spider, a US spider that lives from the southern Midwest through to the Gulf of Mexico, and whose bite, if untreated, may cause tissue damage that lasts several years; and 5) the black widow spider, another North American native whose venom is said to be fifteen times stronger than a rattlesnake's.

What spiders won't eat are bees, wasps and hornets, because they contain venom too.

A spider's hunting style depends on the kind of spider it is. A wolf spider runs after its prey and then pounces on it, like a wolf. The crab spider hides in flowers and grabs insects that land on the flower to feed. But most spiders spin webs. They sit patiently on them and wait for insects to get tangled in their strands. Then it's goodbye insect and hello dinner.

Spider silk is one of the toughest materials on Earth. When it emerges from the spider's spinneret, it's a liquid, but once it's exposed to air, it hardens and becomes stronger than steel. Except, unlike steel, it's flexible; it can stretch up to five times its original length before breaking.

If you live in a city, you'll know that fall is the best time to see spiders, because that's when many species go indoors for warmth and to mate. If you doubt that, check out the cellar or basement of almost any North American house in September or October, and you'll probably see dozens of them. Spiders evolved to live in caves, not houses, but to a spider, a house is like a cave. They're certainly as comfortable as caves, and a whole lot easier to find in a city.

There are thousands of spider species in North America, but as with insects—and mammals and birds and reptiles and amphibians—some adapt better to city living than others. One is the long-legged cellar spider—also known as the daddy longlegs. Not surprisingly, this grayish brown, long-limbed spider lives in cellars and other dark, damp parts of your house, including the crawl space, basement, closets, sink cabinets, garage, attic and shed. Daddy longlegs eat moths,

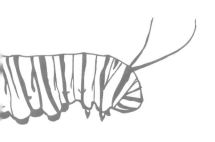

mosquitoes, flies, gnats and beetles they catch in their large raggedy webs. However, in addition to being a cold-blooded killer, the daddy longlegs is a rather sensitive soul—at least as spiders go. If you disturb its web, it will shake so much that its entire web will shake too.

Another familiar city spider is the house spider, named for how common it is in North American homes. This small yellow-brown arachnid (about 1/3 of an inch or 8 millimeters long) will spin its sticky webs almost anywhere under your roof. In fact, if you happen to see a brown hairy spider crawling up the wall of your bedroom, chances are it's a house spider making itself at home. They're also common in bathrooms because they need a fair amount of moisture to survive.

Garden spider is the name given to the family of spiders who spin those delicate dew-covered webs you see on early fall lawns. Garden spiders weave these large flat webs between plants, across paths and between door and window frames. So if you ever have to break through a spider's web to get through a doorway, most likely a garden spider spun it.

Then there's the famous black widow spider. Yes, they live in North American cities, too, providing it isn't too hot.

TOP: Cockroaches are the ultimate urban insects. Wherever people go, cockroaches go too, because they eat so much of the food people throw away. STEPHANIE IP

BOTTOM: Unlike its cousin the garden spider, harvestmen like this one don't have silk glands to produce webs. REBECCA FORSAYETH

ABOVE: Spiders are said to be lucky. That's why you should never kill one. Also, they tend to eat a lot of garden pests. LAURA COX

So Ottawa is a better place to look for one than Austin. And yes, they do bite. Their venom is said to be fifteen times stronger than a rattlesnake's. But black widows are actually quite shy. They don't want to bite you; what they want is to hide from you. So unless you happen to sit on one, there's no reason for humans to be afraid of them—unlike flies, mosquitoes, grasshoppers, caterpillars, beetles or male black widows. When a male finishes mating with a female, she eats him because he serves no further biological purpose. Why do you think they're called black widows?

No discussion of city creepy crawlies would be complete, however, without mentioning the cockroach. If ever there was a consummate insect symbol of big-city living, it's this family of flat-bodied, oval-shaped, long-legged brown or black bugs that almost everyone hates! Whenever someone wants to describe an apartment as unfit for human habitation, the first thing he or she might say is that it's infested with cockroaches. Yet the irony is that cockroaches occupy the places humans

Amazing Animal Adaptation

Some cockroach species have beautiful diaphanous wings. Tinker Bell wouldn't be amiss wearing them. But even wings that beautiful aren't much use when it comes to flying across the country. It's too far and it takes too much effort.

This could explain why, in late 2011, a number of cockroaches decided to take wing in an entirely different way—by airplane. A couple traveling on an AirTran Airways flight from Charlotte to Houston claim they saw a bunch of the insects crawling around their seats. They also say flight attendants did little to get rid of the pesky stowaways when they were pointed out to them. The couple sued the airline for $100,000 in damages, claiming everything from emotional distress to false imprisonment. (Flying these days can feel a little like going to jail.)

This wasn't the first time cockroaches were found aboard a US jet. Earlier the same year about fifty roaches were discovered aboard an American Airlines jet set to take off from Washington. The flight was delayed ninety minutes while flight attendants cleared out the intruders.

An airline representative later said that while infestations are very rare, they're not unprecedented.

live only because we provide them with so much food.

There are more than 5,000 cockroach species worldwide. (The biggest lives in Australia and weighs 50 grams; that's about a Ping-Pong ball's worth of peanut butter.) But regardless of where roaches live or what kind they are, people usually detest them—except perhaps in Cambodia, where they're fried and eaten as snacks.

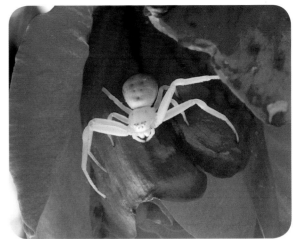

The cockroach is definitely a survivor. In fact, one can live for up to a week without its head. The only reason a headless cockroach finally dies is that it needs its head to drink, and it can only go a week without water. Cockroaches can also go a month without food. However, when they do eat, they eat almost anything. Meat, vegetables, grains or sweets; you serve it and a roach will swallow it. That's why they're so happy living among people. We may hate them, but given the table-groaning smorgasbords we inadvertently lay at their six tiny feet, they must be crazy about us.

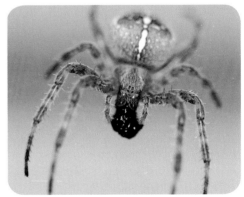

Cockroaches have been around for more than 250 million years, and it's been said that long after the last human has disappeared, they'll still be here. Some scientists reckon even a nuclear blast wouldn't get rid of them. Let's hope we never find out.

In the meantime, wherever humans live, cockroaches won't be far away. For them, a community of humans is a place where food is plentiful and easy to come by. Of course, that's what urban living represents for many forms of wildlife—providing they can take advantage of it. For insects, the trick is to keep away from the creatures who provided the food in the first place—the ones with the heavy feet, the bad attitude and the bug spray.

TOP: The word *spider* comes from an older English word meaning "to spin." DOREEN GRAY

BOTTOM: House spiders are among the most familiar of all urban spiders because they often spin webs in houses. LAURA COX

Conclusion
What We Can Do for Them

This book began by saying it's a hard time to be a wild animal. Indeed, it's hard to imagine a worse time. Who knows how much longer the world's tigers, orangutans and rhinos have? Another fifty years? Another twenty? Tigers may not have even that long. Individual members might linger in zoos and game parks, but where the wild world is concerned, the situation is grim—and getting grimmer all the time. Humans are either crowding large animals out of the places they live, or climate change and other human-induced activities such as pollution and **deforestation** are making it impossible for them to remain where they are. Except they have nowhere else to go. Humans are so overwhelming in terms of both numbers and the way we live that other species have no chance. Even a rhino can't withstand an army.

But urban wildlife is different. As you now know, they're lucky enough to have what it takes to join humans in our conquest of the Earth—or at least not to be done in by it. Although we may have to get used to the terrible prospect of a

OPPOSITE: The natural world is shrinking because there are too many people on the planet. That means there isn't enough room for many of the world's wildlife. MIKE ROGAL/ DREAMSTIME.COM

119

world without tigers, orangutans and rhinos, we probably needn't worry about one without raccoons. Yet even they aren't invulnerable. Animals of every kind can use a helping hand, urban animals included.

Of course, as we saw throughout this book, we already help many city critters without meaning to: by tossing out leftovers, we inadvertently feed pigeons and rats; by growing lush green lawns, we provide dinner to Canada geese and skunks; and by building railways and power lines, we establish travel corridors for snakes. We don't do any of these things with a view to assisting pigeons, geese or snakes; the benefits are accidental. But they're also real. Any harm we do those animals is balanced—at least to some degree—by an unintentional good.

However, there are some conscious steps we can take to help them as well—steps that can make a big difference, yet require little effort. The first requires no effort at all as it's simply to leave them alone. Or at least have as little to do with them as possible: to purposely get away from marine mammals when we're on our boats; to carefully rein in fishing lines when we've used them; and to refrain from deliberately setting out food for wildlife so they won't rely on it the way pets do.

Does that mean we shouldn't have bird feeders? The British Columbia Society for the Prevention of Cruelty to Animals (SPCA), one of a number of groups concerned about the welfare of urban wildlife, won't say. It recognizes that feeders might make winter less arduous for some fragile birds, and it's not about to scold anyone for being kind, but that's it. Generally speaking, when we deliberately put out

food for a wild animal, we disturb nature's balance, and that rarely ends well.

That's why when it comes to other kinds of urban wildlife, the situation is far more cut-and-dried. When we feed raccoons and other urban mammals, we spoil them, and that's not good for anyone. Instead of foraging in a city's green spaces for insects and bird eggs, they'll eat the cat food we leave on our doorsteps and the peanuts we drop in our parks. Why wouldn't they, given that non-human animals like the easy way too? But what happens if we're not there to put out the cat food? What if it's too wet to walk in the park? What will the raccoons eat then? Not only does feeding wild animals make them dependent on us; it gives them a false sense of how much food there is, so they have more babies—too many for the environment to support. But they don't know that, so their population grows in a way nature can't handle.

ABOVE: Black bears can get into camping gear if campsites aren't packed up properly. Then it's time to call a wildlife official, and that's always bad news for the bear. MICHAEL BECKETT

TOP: The sign says it all: *A Fed Bear Is a Dead Bear*. Don't feed the bears.
SARA DUBOIS

BOTTOM: One of the best ways you can help urban wildlife is to plant flowers that attract bees and butterflies.
TESS VAN DONKELAAR

Then disease sets in, and in the wild—even the urban wild—there's no such thing as a veterinarian.

Ideally, we shouldn't feed wild animals accidentally either, but as this book has explained, that's impossible given how much food we throw away. The reason there are so many rats, mice and cockroaches in cities is that we feed them without meaning to all the time. Nevertheless, there are things we can do about that too.

Consider urban bears. When people leave garbage lying around or fail to pick up fruit that falls from their trees, bears will find it. In a year when nature's cupboard is bare, bears will go where they can find food, and depending on where they live, that could be an urban backyard. For some people, a visit from a bear is nothing to get alarmed about; they simply lie low until the bear leaves. But other people panic and reach for their phones. And when conservation officers get involved, there's every chance the bear won't come out alive. So the best thing people who live in bear country can do is not attract them in the first place. They should pick up that fruit and contain that garbage. If bears are hungry, they might still come around, but they won't stick around. And more important, they won't identify that neat fruit-free backyard as a place to return to.

Even if you don't live in bear country, your house can attract other kinds of urban critters. Raccoons, skunks and river otters see attics and basements as potential den sites because they're warm, private and dry—never mind what you think. So if your house isn't sealed properly, what's to stop a family of skunks from moving in? Then it's almost impossible to move them out. You can try scaring them with loud noises and bright lights, but what if that doesn't work? Then it's time to call the exterminator, and that's bound to be bad news for the skunks. A kinder way is to ensure they don't get in in the first place.

On the other hand, when it comes to birds, butterflies and bees, instead of repelling them from our homes and gardens, we should do everything we can to attract them. They're all essential to a healthy environment—especially an urban environment—so when we plant gardens, we should plant them in a way that will make birds, butterflies and bees want to feed, pollinate and lay eggs in them. The best way to do that is to plant native plants—the kinds of plants that grew in your yard before your house was built. Or if you are determined to have plants from elsewhere, make sure they're plants that attract beneficial insects. The choice is almost endless. There are asters, goldenrod, dogwood, buddleia, clover, zinnias, cosmos and many more.

A backyard pond can also be a good place for small reptiles and amphibians. Never mind that it's ornamental; the reptiles and amphibians won't know or care. Once it's dug, you never know when a family of native frogs might decide, like Goldilocks, that it's just right.

It's also important to keep your gardens free of poison. Small urban animals like frogs and birds (not to mention dogs and cats) can easily ingest poisons meant for slugs or snails, and when they do, it's usually lethal. This is why an increasing number of city governments throughout the continent are making pesticide use in urban gardens illegal. If you use organic gardening methods, birds will sing and bees will buzz.

Speaking of birds, what about cats? An often unacknowledged truth is that urban cats wage a devastating war on songbirds. Millions die every year simply because Floyd or Fluffy wants to go hunting. It's not the cats' fault; it's their nature and the

 ## What can you do to protect urban reptiles and amphibians?

First, do what you can to preserve the places where reptiles and amphibians live. If there's a pond in your backyard, look after it. Keep it free of litter, because many small animals, including turtles, can choke on garbage and die. As well, don't use any poisons to kill weeds or insects, because they can poison reptiles and amphibians too. Finally, don't buy exotic species of reptiles and amphibians as pets no matter how "cool" the idea might seem. Reptiles and amphibians don't belong in houses, and when they get released into urban parks and wetlands, they can do serious damage to native plants and wildlife.

ABOVE: Among the many dangers urban wildlife face is discarded fishing line. They can get tangled in it and drown. RABINA PHIPPS

TOP: When you're in the wilderness, remember it's the only home wildlife have. In other words, you're the guest, so act like one. EMILY BROOKS

BOTTOM: Hummingbird feeders may help those tiny birds survive the winter, but when the spring returns, it's time to put them away. LAURA COX

fact that they live in a place they were never meant to be. Domestic cats are descendants of small African wild cats who were domesticated thousands of years ago by ancient Egyptians, who grew to revere them. Now cats are no less doted on in the Western world. But cute and endearing as they are, they remain efficient predators, and terrors to birds.

So how do we stop them from doing what comes naturally? That's a tough question. The obvious answer is to keep them inside. But as anyone who's lived with a cat accustomed to going outside knows, shutting him or her in all of a sudden is almost impossible. However, if a new kitten only knows an indoor environment because it isn't allowed outside, it won't know what it's missing. And the birds will be safe. The SPCA encourages cat owners to build outdoor cages, with perches and quiet areas, so their cats can enjoy fresh air and exercise without hurting wildlife. Spaying or neutering cats is also important, because the fewer there are, the better it is for everyone—the birds *and* the cats. Hundreds of thousands of cats are destroyed in North American shelters each year because there aren't enough homes for them.

Never adopt an exotic pet either. It doesn't matter that many are now bred in captivity in North America. If a snake or bird or lizard wasn't meant to live where you do—if it isn't native to the part of North America where you live—don't take it in…ever. Don't buy exotic pets, don't breed exotic pets and don't set exotic pets free. Think of eastern bullfrogs in Seattle, Burmese pythons in Florida, red-eared slider turtles practically everywhere and the harm they all do. But that's what happens when humans introduce animals to places they shouldn't be: chaos and ruin, over and over again.

Finally, when you visit the wilderness nearest the urban area where you live, remember that, for many kinds of wildlife, it's the only home they have. People are adaptable; they can live almost anywhere. But most wild animals can't. So when you go into a wild animal's home and disturb it with your pickup truck or ATV, there's nowhere for that animal to run except deeper into the same wilderness.

Because people are so powerful, we feel entitled to do whatever we want in nature. We feel entitled to swim in a stream whose edge is browsed by deer. We feel entitled to hike where bears search for berries. We feel entitled to make camp in cougar country. And when a cougar or bear or deer acts in a way we disapprove of, we feel entitled to call a conservation officer with a gun and a team of dogs. Never mind that the cougar or bear or deer has nowhere to run; we feel entitled to hunt him down just the same. The question is: Are we entitled? Do we have the right to act like we own the wilderness too? Wild animals aren't in a position to refuse or welcome us into their homes; we enter regardless. The natural world depends on our goodwill for its survival. The least we can do is make sure we behave ourselves and disturb it as little as possible. Isn't that what any good guest would do?

As you can see, even though ordinary folk may not exercise the same influence on the world as presidents and prime ministers, the decisions we make in our day-to-day lives do matter. The lives and futures of urban wildlife, resilient though they appear, are firmly (or perhaps precariously) in our hands. As we go, so do they. We can either hold on to them for dear life as some of the last precious vestiges of wildlife on this rapidly shrinking and overcrowded planet, or we can selfishly and carelessly let them go. The choice is ours.

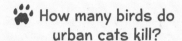

How many birds do urban cats kill?

According to a study done at the University of Wisconsin, North American cat owners estimate their cats catch and kill about one bird a week. The same study suggested there are more than 100 million domestic cats in North America, so you do the arithmetic. But the fact is, no one knows for sure. All we can be sure of is that domestic cats do catch and kill great numbers of songbirds, and that they are partly responsible—along with habitat destruction, climate change, invasive species and city skyscrapers—for the steady decline in the number of urban songbirds in the United States and Canada.

Glossary

adaptation—the process by which animals, including people, adjust to a new environment. Urban wildlife are said to be very adaptive because they can easily change the way they live according to their new surroundings.

carnivore—a dedicated meat eater. Wolves and all large cats are carnivores. Human beings are omnivores, meaning they can eat meat and other kinds of food too.

climate change—the term scientists give to the gradual increase in the temperature of the world's atmosphere, due primarily to an overabundance of carbon dioxide

cold-blooded—animals who rely on their surroundings to dictate their body temperatures. If it's cold outside, they'll be cold too. If it's warm, they'll be comfortable. Fish, reptiles and amphibians are all cold-blooded.

commensal—animals who live close to human beings. Domestic dogs and cats are commensal animals. Rats are too.

conservation officer—government-appointed officials responsible for maintaining the wilderness and the wildlife in that wilderness. Unfortunately, conservation officers are often called upon to kill wildlife who are considered dangerous to human beings.

deforestation—the destruction of a forest by either human or natural means, such as logging or wildfire

displacement—the process that occurs when a new species is introduced to an environment and it begins to take over the breeding sites and feeding grounds of a species that was already there.

ecology—the study of the relationships between living organisms and their environments

ecosystem—a community of plants and animals living together within a particular physical environment

exoskeleton—an external skeleton. Mammals, birds, fish, reptiles and amphibians all have internal skeletons, meaning they're contained within the animal's skin and muscle structure. An insect's exoskeleton takes the place of its skin. It not only protects the insect's internal organs; it also helps define the insect's shape.

extinction—the elimination of a species to the point that it has disappeared from the Earth forever. The dinosaurs are extinct. About a quarter of all the world's large mammals are expected to be extinct by the end of this century.

exurb—settlements beyond the suburbs of a city. When a city stretches out from its center, it stretches first into suburbs, then exurbs.

food chain—the direct link between species according to what—and whom—they eat. Little fish eat plankton. Bigger fish eat the little fish. And sharks eat the big fish. This is a food chain.

generalist—animals who don't require specific foods or a specific kind of environment to survive. They are animals who can eat a wide variety of foods and live in different kinds of homes. Raccoons, coyotes, rats and pigeons are all generalists.

habitat—the specific environment in the wild where an animal lives

habitat degradation—the continual decline in quality of a habitat, caused by pollution, industrial development or something else

intertidal zone—the area along the seashore where the tide comes in and goes out. When the tide is in, the intertidal zone is underwater. When the tide is out, it's open to the air.

invasive species—plants or animals that don't belong in a particular environment. Human beings often introduce invasive species either deliberately or accidentally into habitats where they don't belong. Burmese pythons set free in the Florida Everglades are a particularly destructive form of invasive species.

migration—when birds or other kinds of animals travel from one part of the world to another, usually for feeding and breeding. Geese, ducks, monarch butterflies and gray whales are all migrating species in that they spend their summers in the northern half of the world and their winters farther south, where it's warm. An animal who migrates is called a *migrator*.

native species—plants or animals that live and grow naturally in a particular habitat or environment. Grizzly bears living in the rainforest are native to that rainforest.

overfishing—refers to excessive or reckless fishing in a particular area, often leading to a decline in fish populations

predator—an animal who hunts another animal

prey—an animal that is hunted by another animal

raptor—birds who hunt other birds for food. Eagles, hawks, falcons and owls are all raptors. Also known as birds of prey.

salt marsh—wet, boggy places where freshwater rivers meet the salty sea. The water in salt marshes isn't fresh; nor is it as salty as seawater. The term used to describe it is *brackish*.

specialist—an animal who requires a highly specific diet or a particular kind of habitat to survive. Ninety-nine percent of a panda's diet is composed of bamboo leaves, making the panda one of nature's specialists.

urban ecology—refers to environments within an urban area that support wild animals and plants. When scientists speak of green spaces or other areas within cities and how they sustain different kinds of wildlife, they are speaking of the urban ecology of those places.

urban ocean—the area that lies directly offshore from coastal urban areas, as well as the ocean that feeds into cities. Shipping lanes are part of the urban ocean because ships that supply cities with much of what they need to function use the lanes to get in and out of ports.

urban wildlife—refers to animals that have adapted to live and even thrive in cities and other urban environments

warm-blooded—animals who have an internal mechanism for regulating their body temperatures. Mammals and birds are warm-blooded which means that if the air or water temperature around them is neither too high nor low, their body temperature will stay the same.

wetland—the generic name given to places like marshes, bogs and swamps. Generally speaking, the soil in wetlands is constantly moist and consequently will only support the growth of certain kinds of plants and animals.

Resources

Bear Aware
www.bearaware.bc.ca/be-bear-aware

Humane Society
www.humanesociety.org/animals/wild_neighbors
www.humanesociety.org/animals/resources/urban_wildlife_sanctuary_program
    .html#id=album-28&num=content-487

People for the Ethical Treatment of Animals (PETA)
www.peta.org/issues/wildlife/default.aspx

Society for the Prevention of Cruelty to Animals (SPCA)
www.spca.bc.ca/welfare/wildlife/urban-wildlife

Urban Habitats
http://urbanhabitats.org/index.html

Urban Nature Information Service
http://unis.mcgill.ca/en/uw/index.html

Urban Park Rangers
www.nycgovparks.org/sub_about/parks_divisions/urban_park_rangers/pd_ur.html
www.nycgovparks.org/kids

Urban Wildlife Institute
www.lpzoo.org/conservation-science/science-centers/urban-wildlife-institute

Urban Wildlife Society
www.urbanwildlifesociety.org/UWS

Urban Wildlife "The Humane Approach"
www.urbanwildlife.ca

US Census Bureau Population Clock
www.census.gov/main/www/popclock.html

Wildlife Conservation Society
www.wcs.org

World Changing
www.worldchanging.com/archives/008715.html

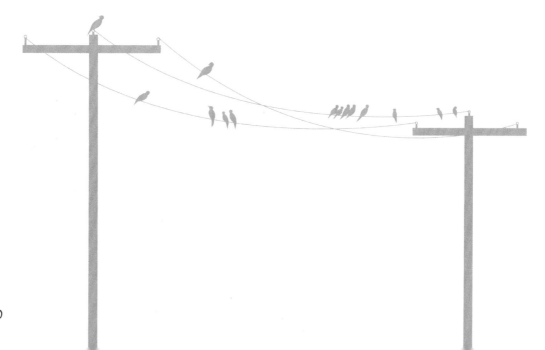

Index

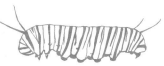

Page numbers in **bold** refer to images.

Acknowledgments

This book could not have been written without the knowledge, expertise and generosity of people who study and work with urban wildlife every day. Thanks to them, I was able to gain an understanding of the subject myself. But without their original research, inquisitiveness and hard work, this book would not exist. I am indebted to them. They are:

John Calambokidis, Co-founder, Cascadia Research Collective, Olympia, Washington

Wayne Campbell, Bird Biologist and Former Curator of Ornithology at the Royal British Columbia Museum in Victoria, British Columbia

C. J. Casson, Curator of Life Sciences, Seattle Aquarium, Seattle, Washington

Sara Dubois, Manager of Wildlife Services, British Columbia Society for the Prevention of Cruelty to Animals, Vancouver, British Columbia

Stan Gehert, Associate Professor and Wildlife Extension Specialist, School of Environment and Natural Resources, Ohio State University, Columbus, Ohio

Chris Harley, Assistant Professor, Department of Zoology, University of British Columbia, Vancouver, British Columbia

Morgan Hocking, NSERC Post-Doctorate, Department of Biological Sciences, Simon Fraser University, Burnaby, British Columbia

Darren Julian, Urban Wildlife Specialist, Arizona Department of Fish and Game, Mesa, Arizona

Amy Knowlton, Research Scientist, New England Aquarium, Boston, Massachusetts

Eric Lonsdorf, Former Director, Urban Wildlife Institute, Chicago, Illinois

Gary Luck, Assistant Professor, Institute for Land, Water and Society, Charles Stuart University, New South Wales, Australia

Barry Kent MacKay, Writer, Natural History Specialist, and Founding Director of Zoocheck Canada and Species Survival International, Toronto, Ontario

Seth Magle, Director, Urban Wildlife Institute, Chicago, Illinois

Julia Phillips, Adopt-a-Pond Coordinator, Toronto Zoo, Toronto, Ontario

Tom Pitchford, Wildlife Biologist, Florida Fish and Wildlife Conservation Commission, Jacksonville, Florida

Richard Simon, Deputy Director, Urban Park Rangers, New York City, New York

Ann Spellman, Marine Mammal Biologist, Marine Mammal Section, Florida Fish and Wildlife Conservation Commission, St. Petersburg, Florida

Tony Young, Florida Fish and Wildlife Conservation Commission, Tallahassee, Florida

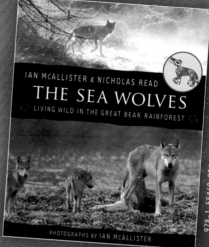

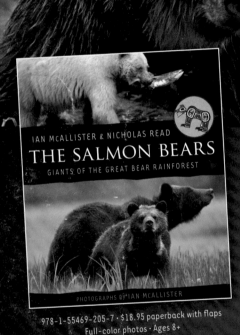